Computer Literacy
Made Easy ... And Fun

Bits, Bytes, Apples and Mice

S0-ACC-919

Computer Literacy Made Easy ... And Fun

Bits, Bytes, Apples and Mice

James R. Callan

Illustrated by Arthur Winner

Pennant Publishing, Winnsboro, Texas

Computer Literacy Made Easy ... And Fun
Bits, Bytes, Apples and Mice

By James R. Callan

Published by: Pennant Publishing
PO Drawer 25
Winnsboro, Texas 75494-0025
Printed and bound in the United States of America

Publisher's Cataloging in Publication
Callan, James R.
    Computer literacy made easy .. and fun: bits, bytes, Apples and mice / James R. Callan ; illustrated by Arthur Winner
    p. cm.
    includes index
    ISBN   0-9646850-3-5 : $12.95
    1. Computer literacy. 2. Computers. I. Title
QA76.9.C64C35 1995   004
                                       QBI95-20236
Library of Congress Catalog Card Number: 95-69488

Table of Contents

Acknowledgments

A special thanks to **Kelly Callan** for her work early in this project to show that cartoons could add to the readability of this subject. Thanks also to **Diane Bailey** and **Kristi Callan** for their contributions, and to **Dr. Jamie Callan** for his comments on the state of computing. **Charlie McDonald**, at a Kinko's, provided cheerful help with some of the problems of laying out the cover in color on a computer. And another special thanks goes to my wife for her support and good humor throughout this project.

While I have received help from a number of people, any errors which found their way into this book are mine (or maybe caused by a virus lurking in my computer).

Disclaimer

If you're buying this book so that it will make you a computer programmer, or an authority, or even an expert on spread sheets, it is the wrong book. This book is designed to make you familiar with much of the language of computers, to allow you to understand much of what people are talking about when they are talking casually about computers. If two computer hackers are in a deep discussion about the internal workings of either the hardware or the software, you probably still won't follow what they are talking about. But, you should be able to follow the computer stories on the evening news or in the daily papers or the news and business magazines. You should be able to follow much of the "computer talk" that authors include in fiction. You should be able to understand most of what kids, spouse and friends are talking about when the topic centers around computers. In some cases, you'll know more than they do, and won't be plagued with false ideas. You'll be ... computer literate. Not an expert. And if you're about to take a first course on a computer topic of almost any sort, this book should help you.

The information in this book has been checked for accuracy. However, the computer field is changing so rapidly that it is impossible to insure that everything is perfectly up-to-date. In just the time between writing, printing and distributing this book, many new developments will have taken place. The basics are here, if not the latest wrinkle.

Computer Literacy Made Easy...
And Fun

Bits, Bytes, Apples and Mice

Introduction

When my kids were young, if I heard "bit" or "bite", I knew there was a fight going on. Nowadays, even first graders are talking about bits and bytes and lan servers in friendly tones.

We are a product of our times, and today's children are growing up in the technology era. Computers are everywhere and they do everything from helping children learn to talk, to handling our bank accounts. They monitor the temperature in our cars, write us "personal" notes, keep the microwave oven on track and adjust the traffic lights (so that they'll be red when we arrive at the intersection); they monitor milk production of cows, diagnose illnesses, draw plans for our homes, figure our taxes, entertain us, process our photographs, and call us on the phone to make sales pitches.

Like it or not, computers are only going to become more entrenched (some might say entangled) in our lives.

Now, I'm going to assume that you don't know much about computers—and maybe don't plan to use one. But you *would* like to know what your spouse, child or friend is talking about. Not to mention Tom Clancy and other authors, or the people on "Donohue." At the very least, you'd like to know whether they're talking shop or being nasty. So, in this book (written by a human, but typeset by ... you guessed it ... a computer) I'll define some of those mysterious words. I'll try to make the concepts and definitions easy to understand — despite the continuous efforts of some of my colleagues to restrict the circle of cognoscente (those in the know).

A quick aside, just to make you feel better. In the 50's, the head of one of the major companies in the young computer field predicted that, while computers were wonderful, the market in the U.S. would be only a few dozen. Total!

I will "boldface" terms when I define them. And I've included an index. So if a friend says John is a *hacker*, or Mary is into *AI*, just look in the index and it will lead you to a quick explanation of what she's saying. But right now, just start reading and soon you'll know what the **Techies** (people who are caught up in technology) are really talking about. You'll find out why someone saying "I put a mouse on my toaster" makes perfect sense to computer aficionados.

Petite - or 42 regular?

There are all sorts of ways to categorize computers. Here's one: computers are either small, medium or large. Pretty easy, huh? But computer people like to use their own language so that the rest of us will be impressed. (It's like when I was young; the kid with the secret decoder ring had an edge on the rest of us.  He knew the definitions, so to speak.) Anyway, the computer people call them micros, minis, and mainframes. Now you tell me; is that better than small, medium and large?

Microcomputers, or **micros**, as they're usually called, are the small computers that you see everywhere: in Sears, Radio Shack, lots of homes, and first grade class rooms. If a micro is light enough to carry easily, and can run on a battery, it's called a **portable**. If it's small enough, it's called a **lap top**; even smaller, a **notebook computer.** (These really are about the size of a notebook.)

Micros are often called **personal computers**. Not because they get personal, but because they are generally used only by one person—at a time. So a person can say "This is my PERSONAL computer". Lap tops and notebooks are very popular because they are status symbols. Almost as good as a car phone. Especially in an airport. You carry one of those babies on and people think, "This guy is important. He has his OWN, PERSONAL computer." If you had a mini-computer, or a mainframe (which cost a <u>lot</u> more), you couldn't do that. Not a single soul in the airport would even *know* that you had a computer of your own. However, the thing for you to know is: all of these—personal, portable, laptop, notebook—are <u>micros</u>.

There are also **hand-held** or **palmtop computers**. But at 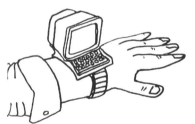 press time they are still not really important. They're like the 3" TV: cute, but do you really want to use it? So I'm just going to ignore them. Today. But with improved wireless transmission, you could use one to send mail, or get a stock price while you were walking through the park.

Minicomputers, or **minis**, are bigger than micros. Too big to carry. They don't run on batteries, you don't see them in Sears and you can't take them on the plane. But they still aren't *really* big. Bigger than a bread box, smaller than the fridge. Oh, and they cost more money than the micros and can do more.

Mainframes. It just sounds big. Like it should be in all capitals, as in **M A I N F R A M E S**. You almost want to say it with a deep voice. These insist on a private room. Air conditioning in both summer <u>and</u> winter! They cost big dollars, too. And they're definitely not personal. Generally, many people—hundreds, maybe—use a mainframe simultaneously. This is the type that the IRS uses to keep track (I'm being polite, here) of our money.

Mainframes actually came first. Then, when someone built a smaller and less powerful computer, they called it the minicomputer. And when an even smaller one came along, it became the microcomputer.

While all three types are still very much in use today, you can think of the 1950's and 60's as the mainframe decades; the 70's and 80's as the hey-days of the minicomputers; and the 80's and 90's as the micro years. And the progress has been phenomenal. You can buy a micro with 2,000 of today's dollars and have a much more powerful and reliable machine than you could have had for $5 million in 1955. And instead of needing a special building with temperature and humidity control, anti-static devices and special electrical circuits as the 1955 machine did, today's micro is carry-on luggage that you can use in the airplane as it cruises along at 35,000 feet.

The inside story

Most of the computers in the world are micros, so we'll concentrate on those. However, a lot of what we say applies to the bigger computers, anyway. And we don't want to get hung up on the technical difficulties.

The heart of the micro computer is the **Motherboard**. So if you hear your son say "That's a big motherboard," don't scold him. This mother is a thin, rectangular piece of fiber glass with many electronic components attached to one side. On the other side it has silver lines, lots of them. These are simply electrical wires molded to the board, which is a lot neater than having loose wires hanging around.

Why is it called a Motherboard? Everything comes from it— it is the <u>mother</u> of all operations in the computer! In a micro, it's also the biggest board. Big Mamma!

Many of the thingamajigs (components) on the top of the motherboard are called **chips**. They're also called **IC's** (short for **I**ntegrated **C**ircuits, which we'll discuss in a later chapter entitled "Chips and dips.") These are small, plastic pieces anywhere from a half inch to two inches long and, except for the really important ones, less than a half inch wide. They're usually a nice charcoal gray, and often have white printing on them that is too small to read—unless you have the eyes of a teenager. All of them, even the important ones, are only about a quarter of an inch thick. Coming out of the longer sides and curving down are lots of silver strips. If you see an IC not mounted on a board, these silver strips look like legs on a gray bug. All it really needs are antennae.

The biggest IC, or Chip, is usually the **microprocessor**. (If there are two big ones, the second one is probably a **co-processor**—sort of like a co-pilot.) The microprocessor has the most legs, but it's really the brain. It does all the thinking, all the adding, subtracting, dividing, and deciding. And it tells the rest of the stuff what to do—and when to do it. The big cheese, so to speak. They could call it The Boss , The Brain or Queen "B", but instead they call it the **CPU**, short for **C**entral **P**rocessing **U**nit. The co-processor, like the co-pilot, might be nearly as capable as the microprocessor, but still does what it's told to do.

Many of today's computer controlled products only require the microprocessor chip. There's probably a microprocessor in your microwave, your VCR, any new TV, and several in your car. They are even found in some kids' toys—the expensive ones.

Back on the motherboard, some of the chips are **memory chips**. These can hold information while the machine is turned on. Turn the computer off and the memory goes blank. Like Uncle Willie: when he went to sleep, he forgot everything, including the roller skates he had promised me.

The memory chips, or simply **The Memory**, can "remember" the operating system and programs (we'll define those under software, and we'll define software under software) and **data**. Data is simply information: numbers, names, any-  thing worth keeping track of, and often a lot of stuff that's *not* worth keeping track of.

If you want some examples of data, read this paragraph; if not, skip to the next chapter. Data for a bank computer is information on the checks you write and the deposits you make, loans the bank makes and payments it gets, plus information to make up its payroll and pay its taxes. In a school's computer, the grades, attendance records, and teachers' schedules are data. For the phone company, data includes information on the numbers you called, when you called and how long you talked.

Data is simply information that someone wants to keep track of. It helps if it's organized. But that's not necessary; it's still data.

An aside: the word data is plural, and we should really write "Data are ...". But most of us are accustomed to hearing "Data is ...". So, I'll take that liberty and hope my English teacher doesn't read this.

OK. I turned it on. Now what?

When you turn the computer on, the memory is blank. (Well, how is your memory when you wake up?) But there are a couple of those small chips that *do* remember things. These are called **BIOS** chips. BIOS stands for **B**asic **I**nput **O**utput System. These BIOS chips are **ROM**'s—which means **R**ead **O**nly **M**emory. They're sort of like an expensive book that you can read as often as you wish but that you can't write in. The BIOS knows how to feed information into the computer's memory so the computer can work.

The regular memory is called **RAM**, for **R**andom **A**ccess **M**emory. It's like a chalkboard; you can write anywhere on it you want, read it, erase it, change it; but at the end of the day (whenever the computer is turned off) the chalk board gets wiped clean. RAM is pronounced as a single word, not three letters. The same is true for ROM.

The BIOS puts an **Operating System** into the computer's memory and now the computer is able to do some work. The Operating System runs the show. You might think of the **OS** (Operating System) as an office manager: it makes the pieces work together, determines what it is that needs to be done and sees that it gets done. Oh, you pronounce OS as two letters, O and S.

What does the computer run?

It **runs** (or executes or performs) a **program**. A Program is simply a series of instructions, telling the computer what to do - like add up numbers, or print out letters (more likely *bills*), or send a fax or check your oil. Some person (called a programmer—see the chapter *Bugs and Hackers*) wrote down the instructions on how to accomplish a certain task, fed them into the computer and gave the set of  instructions a name, such as WRITEMOM. These instructions might tell the computer how to crank out a weekly letter to your mother. Now, if you ask the computer to execute WRITEMOM, it will follow those instructions to the letter. (Of course the pun was intended!) If the instructions were well-thought out and well-written, you get what you want; if they were not, you get ... who knows what?

Of course, many programs a computer runs are complicated things, like a program to guide a space probe, or a program to help design a nuclear sub, or one of the new sophisticated computer games. These require a huge collection of instructions, tens or hundreds of thousands of instructions. In the case of a space probe or a nuclear sub, the programs must consider every possibility, and allow for no error. One wrong instruction could be very costly.

The Operating System, mentioned above, is also a program, albeit a special one. It coordinates all the activities in the computer—sort of like a traffic cop at a busy intersection.
Let me depart for a minute. First, what is a file? A computer **file** is a collection of data which has a name and is stored on a disk. You're right. I haven't defined a disk yet. For now, think of it as a type of memory that doesn't forget when the power goes off. More details in the next chapter. Anyway, the computer keeps track of where that data is stored and you can access it by using the name you've given the file.

The computer file could hold a set of instructions to execute, like the WRITEMOM program mentioned above. Or it could be a collection of numbers, such as the checks you wrote last month. A micro can hold all the checks the parents can write, plus all the telephone calls a teenager can make.

If you wanted the computer to run WRITEMOM, you would simply type in just that one word— WRITEMOM. The computer would look for this file and when it found it, read the instructions and follow 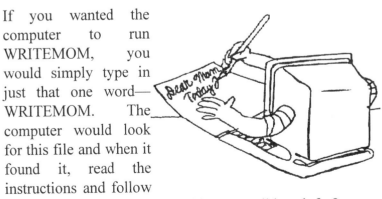 them exactly. What more could you possibly ask for?

Or suppose you typed in a list of all your checks for the month of February and asked the computer to store it in a file on the disk and give that file the name CHECKS.FEB . If later you wanted to use that information, you would simply ask for the file by name—CHECKS.FEB . The computer would search the disk until it found that file. We'll talk about the intelligence of a computer later, but I will tell you right now that the computer manages to keep track of things much, much better than I can. It rarely loses things, and it finds files in an instant. It's just better organized than I am. No Fibber McGee's closet here.

Before we leave the notion of files, I might mention two kinds of files. Not that you really care—the computer will worry about that. But, because some of the people you rub elbows with (I never could figure why you'd want to rub elbows with anyone) will use these terms, I'll mention them. First, there are **ASCII** files. We'll define ASCII later but for now, these are files that we humans can read. And there are

THE BLOB

binary files (also defined later) which only the computer can read. And guess what they call a really big binary file? A **BLOB**. That's for **B**inary **L**arge **OB**ject. Perhaps some computer people do have a sense of humor, even if it escapes us most of the time. Maybe they keep their humor in a binary file and we can't read it.

Directories

As you can imagine, after a while you and the computer accumulate a lot of files. And like recipes or tax papers, you need to organize them. On a computer, you can divide file storage into **Directories** and put your files in these to help you keep track. You could think of the disk as a file cabinet and the directories as file drawers. Then each disk file could be considered a file folder with data in it. You organize these folders into the drawers in a way that makes sense to you.

One directory (file drawer), for instance, might be called "Hometax" while another could be "Games" and still another "Letters". All the tax info goes into the hometax directory. All your game programs would go in the game directory, and your correspondence would go in the letters directory. Or you could set up a hierarchy, if you wish. For instance, you could have a directory called "Personal" and it could have sub-directories for "Hometax", "Games", and "Letters."

The base directory of a disk, the one that's there *before* you create any directories, is called the **root directory** of the disk. And if someone says "Get a directory", they don't mean take one, but rather they mean get a list of the names of the files that are stored in a particular directory.

Pat yourself on the back. You already know as much as a lot of people who use computers all the time.

Disks and crashes!

What happens when the computer is turned off? As we said earlier, the memory (RAM) goes blank. The ROM remembers what it knows, but that isn't much.

So how do we keep those programs and files around? In the old days, we kept them on cards with holes punched in them. The computer's card reader would read those holes and translate the holes into information. Nowadays, we store the information on **disks**, mostly. So what's a disk? Well, it's shaped like a disk—round and thin. Looks kind of like an old phonograph record—without the grooves. It has a thin coat of a material that can store information, in much the same way as your tape recorder can store your voice or a song. Not exactly, but sort of. The disk is in some protective covering, so you see the rectangular plastic or metal housing.

The good news is, information stored on a disk doesn't go away when the computer is turned off. If there's something in RAM (random access memory) worth keeping, we give it a unique name and tell the computer to copy it to a disk, before we turn the computer off.

Since information can be stored on a disk and the disk remembers it, some people call disks **secondary memory**, or **long term memory**, or **disk memory**, or **hard memory** or **permanent memory**. As we'll see later, it isn't exactly permanent. But then, what is? My wife gets a permanent, but it doesn't last very long.

Disks

Data and programs can be saved on these disks. Some of the disks hold a great deal of information—tens of millions of words or numbers. These are called **hard disks**. They're "hard" disks not because there's so much information that it's "hard" to find anything, but simply because the disk itself is made of hard, rigid metal which has been coated with a material that can be selectively magnetized. Hard disks are generally **non-removable**, meaning they're inside the computer and you keep your hands off. (I say generally; there are a few hard disks that you can remove and carry from home to office or city to city.)

Today's disks are a real paradox: each year, the disks being manufactured are smaller than the ones made the year before, but, can store <u>more</u> information. The information that you can store on one of today's disk drives that you can hold in the palm of your hand would have required a disk drive 15 years ago the size of a washing machine.

How much will one of these small disks hold? It varies a lot. But you can set a disk in the palm of your hand that will hold

500 million characters (letters or numbers). To give that a little perspective, let's say that you could store every word of 700 to 1,000 best-selling novels on one hard disk. Oh yes, there are some hard disks—most, actually—that hold a lot less information; they generally cost less, but have about the same physical dimensions. A typical hard drive on a new micro today might be in the 250 to 500 megabyte (million character) range. Just two years ago 80 to 120 megabytes was typical.

It's necessary to mention the "hard" part in hard disks because there are also **floppy disks**. On these, the disk on which the data is actually recorded is flexible. They don't hold nearly as much information and they're slower than hard disks. But they are small, cheap, can be removed from the computer and even sent through the mail—and survive! Floppies are also called **diskettes**.

While the hard disk is meant to stay in the computer, the floppy is meant to go in and out and be passed around. So, hard disk and hard disk drive are pretty synonymous, since you don't separate them. But the floppy disk is distinct from the floppy drive. You have a floppy drive on your computer. Then you buy dozens, maybe hundreds of floppy disks. And you put in one of those when you need something that's on the floppy disk, or you want to transfer a file from the computer to the diskette. Analogous to a tape cassette and a tape player. This is the usual way for

moving programs and data around. When you buy a software package, it comes on a floppy or diskette.

Back to the best-selling novels, a diskette can hold between 1 and 4 books. Well, I did say they were cheap!

The complete device, including the motor to turn the disk (it spins like a phonograph record), the electronics, the "read" and "write" heads and the housing, is called a **disk drive**, If you want to get specific, you could specify a **hard disk drive** or a **floppy** or **diskette drive**.

Data is stored on disks using a system of 0's and 1's. A "1" is stored by magnetizing a tiny spot on the disk. A zero is stored by not magnetizing the spot. So a disk that could hold just a million characters would need eight million microscopic spots that it could either magnetize or not magnetize. It needs eight million because it takes eight of these spots to represent each character. It's a little like Morse Code, which uses two symbols: a dot and a dash. By using these in combination, you can send any letter or number you want. The computer uses 0's and 1's instead of dots and dashes—and uses its own coding scheme. But the idea of coding information using only two symbols is the same.

The disks we've talked about so far are magnetic disks. There are also **laser** or **optical disks**. These are slower than hard disks—that is, it takes longer to retrieve a file from a laser disk than it does from a magnetic hard disk. But they pack the data even tighter, so you can get more data per square inch on a laser disk than on a magnetic disk. For instance, you can buy a complete, 20 volume encyclopedia on a single laser disk. And it might include a number of short videos (moving pictures with sound) to enliven some of the historical segments. Plus, of course, it will have an excellent indexing and lookup system. All on one 5" optical disk.

Usually, these are called **CD-ROM**'s, for **Compact Disk, Read Only Memory**. Like the diskette, these CD-ROMs can be removed from the CD-ROM drive and sent through the mail or carried over to a neighbor's house.

These disks look and operate like the CD (Compact Disk) that you buy music on today. They are great for storing lots of data and they are not too expensive. But like the music CD's, recording on them *is* expensive. So mostly they are used to read data that has been put on laser disks that you buy.

However, the price of laser disks that you can write on is coming down. Before long, even home computers will have optical disks that you can both read *and* write. But unless you want to write an awful lot of stuff, the magnetic disks are a better bet. The magnetic disk is generally about 25 times faster than a CD-ROM.

Can you store information on a tape like your audio cassette tape recorder? Well, just about. The tape looks about the same, but it operates a little differently. And of course it requires a computer **tape drive** to read and write the tapes. Tapes can hold a lot of data and are not very fragile, so they are good for mailing. Since tapes are slow, they aren't usually used for your main working storage. But, they're excellent for **backup,** which means extra copies of your files just in case the computer erases its disks.

Gadzooks!

Would the computer *really* erase its disks?

It can and does happen. Which brings up a very important term. **Crash.** The computer can crash, which means fail. If crash sounds more dramatic and drastic than fail, it should. A computer looks at a crash like a city looks at an earthquake. It can be minor, just a small tremor on the computer's Richter scale, and the computer loses what it was doing and has to be restarted. Or it can be a major crash for the computer, like a 6.4 earthquake for the city. You might lose something really important and the computer won't even start again and you have to call in a repairman and you're **Down** (the computer won't run—see the next chapter) for three days. Or it can be catastrophic, like an 8.2 Richter scale earthquake. This means you lose a disk, which means you lose all the data on the disk. That is often the result of a **head crash**, where one of the heads that reads and writes on the disk comes crashing down on the surface of the disk and damages it. Without a back-up, you could lose months of work.

Could a faulty program, or a virus, erase data from a disk? Yes. Doesn't happen often. But it does happen. Can a person accidentally erase one, some, or all files in a directory? He sure can. And that happens much more often than head crashes. Of course the person will blame it on the computer. As of today, most computers cannot defend themselves against libel.

Sorry, the computer's down

Those are among the most discouraging words known. They tell you nothing, except that whatever it is you wanted, you're not getting under any circumstances. And there is no known time when it might be done.

I sometimes suspect businesses that tell me "the computer's down," don't even have a computer. But what a great excuse. You can speak to the supervisor, but if the computer's down, what can she do? Nothing

But if this is for real, what does it mean?

Generally it means a problem with the computer hardware has occurred. And if they're telling the truth about the crash, they're telling the truth when they say they don't know when it will be fixed.

We mentioned computer crashes and head crashes earlier. When a crash happens, first everyone screams and curses. Have you ever noticed that computer people shudder whenever the lights blink—even at your house where there is no computer? That's because they know that even the slightest power interruption can bring a computer down.

Often that just means that whatever was being done at the time is lost. But sometimes, because the computer was operating on some particular file at the moment of the power loss, it could trash that file. And of course, when the computer is shut down so unceremoniously, there could be hardware damage as well.

Finding the problem can be quite a task in itself. It's like when your TV goes out. If it goes out and stays out, there's a chance that the repair man can find the problem and fix it. But if it goes out sporadically, it's much harder. You know how it always seems to happen. We (that's the detective and I) are opening the door to discover the murderer and ... only white static shows up on the TV. We have a beautiful color picture for the commercial to start the next program; but we'll never know "who done it". Or, there are five seconds to go in the game, your team is behind by six points but on the four yard line. Black screen. The TV comes back on *just* in time for the commercial *after* the game.

So, maybe the problem in the computer can be found in a reasonable time (never quickly) and maybe not. Either way, the repairman will have every spare part known to mankind—except the one that went bad. In fact, he will swear that particular part has never before failed in the history of civilization. This failure will probably go into the Guinness Book of Records.

Then again, the problem could be a software crash. (Software is a set of instructions telling the computer what to do.) If that's the case, the computer might simply re-start. Of course, it's likely that some crucial program—most likely the one that affects you—won't run. You get the same answers when you phone for help, and the same results just as if it were a hardware crash. In fact, they may not even *know* whether the problem is hardware or software! That's even worse. It brings up another typical situation: the hardware repairman says it's a software problem, and the software people are sure it's a hardware problem. So neither wants to spend any time trying to fix it. They *might* find the problem today. But if they do, *they* will be in the Guinness book.

Of course, "The computer's down", might just mean that Susan is home sick today and as soon as she gets back you can get your answer.

What causes a crash?

There are lots of things that can cause a crash. A person bumping the computer while the disk is active could make the disk head crash into the disk itself, and cause damage. This is not as likely today as it was a few years back. Most crashes are caused by one of three things. (1) A fluctuation in the electrical power coming into the computer could cause a minor crash (failure). Of course, a power surge *could* fry the whole computer. Lightening strikes nearby have been known to send such a surge through the power lines.

(2) Mistakes (called **bugs**) in software can cause the system to crash. If a situation arises where the instructions don't make sense, the computer may, figuratively, throw up its hands in desperation, i.e. crash. We'll talk about software several times before we finish.

(3) Failure of some electronic component is the most likely cause of a crash. It could be as simple as the fan that cools the power supply. If the fan stops, the power supply gets too hot and the system crashes. The computer has thousands of electronic components. They are all very reliable. But if one fails, even briefly, even for one thousandth of a second, the system will probably crash.

How likely is a computer to fail? Depends on the computer, how much it is used and under what conditions. But let's suppose, just for sake of argument, that my computer has 1,000 components that could fail. And let's say that each one might fail, on average, just once in 100 years. That makes, on average, ten failures each year—nearly one per month. Most micros do not have any where near that many hardware failures. So, you see, the components are very reliable. Even as computers become more complicated, they are also becoming more reliable. Particularly the hardware. But they do fail occasionally.

Frequently, you can predict when the computer will fail. If you really need to get something done, there is a higher likelihood of failure than if you are not pressed at all. Murphy was undoubtedly a computer user, and Murphy's law was probably formed while he was sitting in front of a monitor.

Bits and Bytes

The subtitle mentioned bits and bytes so maybe we should discuss them. A **Bit** is the basic unit of information that the computer understands and stores. A Bit is like a light switch: it's either on or it's off. The com-

Bit

puter takes that to mean either a 1 or a 0. On is 1. Off is 0. That's really all the computer understands! 0's and 1's. So much for a smart machine. So humans must translate everything into 0's and 1's for the computer. The name Bit comes from **BI**nary digi**T**—binary meaning two, and digit meaning a character in a number system: in this case, a two character system. With the decimal system, as kids we counted on our (ten) fingers. With the binary system, we would count on just our thumbs.

Remember when we talked about the disks storing only 0's and 1's? It stores Bits (**BI**nary digi**TS**). Magnetize the spot, it's a 1. Don't magnetize the spot, it's a 0.

To store info in the computer, we string together lots of these 0's and 1's. Some of these strings of bits, or **bit strings**, get very long. If we worked in binary and were writing checks, for example, we would have to write the year 1995 as 11111001011. (Appendix A explains this.)

Bits are often organized into groups of eight. Each group is called a **Byte**. A byte can hold one character—for example: A, m, &, *, +, $—in some coding systems; or it could hold a number, between 0 to 255, in binary form (not as characters).

Byte

Of course, most computer users never deal with bits. Or bytes. A computer program handles the translation for them. But that's what the computer works with, and *some* computer people do have to deal with bits and bytes all the time.

Here's one that not even all the computer people know. If I ask you what a **Nibble** is, you'd probably say it's a small bite. You're right! A nibble is four bits—half a byte.

Computer people also like to talk about **Megabytes** (a million bytes) and **Kilobytes** (a thousand bytes). The amount of storage on disks and tapes, and in the memory, is generally given in kilobytes or megabytes. So if a friend says "I just got my 300 meg drive" that translates to "I just got a hard disk drive that can hold 300 million characters of information." Or "That file is 400K" means the file is 400,000 bytes long. In print, these often look like 300MB and 400KB. MB stands for MegaByte, KB for KiloByte. **Gigabyte** (a billion character) disks are becoming more common, and some large applications may need storage for a **Terabyte** (a trillion bytes) of information, requiring several disk drives.

... And Apples

With all this talk about bits and bytes, food had to come up. An **Apple** is a particular brand of microcomputer. The company is named **Apple Computer, Inc.** Many of its computers are "Apples". They also have a very successful series of machines called **Macintosh**. There's a rumor that they may be coming out with a new computer called Golden Delicious ...

Why Apple? Why Guess? jeans? Why Saturn cars? Somebody liked the name.

While we're on food, there are also Apricot Computers. And Peachtree Software, Orange Micro and Orange Systems, Radisys (well, it almost sounds like radish), and to decorate the table, Orchid. I've heard people say they had a lemon, but I don't know whether that had a capital L or not. I haven't seen a Broccoli Computer—yet.

Apple deserves a lot of credit for shifting the microcomputer industry into high gear. They proved that people would buy these new small machines. The company actually started in a garage and within a few years was a billion dollar corporation. The stuff dreams—and computer stories—are made of.

IBM has been a giant in the computer field for decades. Their first micro was called simply **PC**—for personal computer, I guess. IBM had been selling only the million dollar babies before, so they might have named it PC for Pretty Cheap, since the PC cost only a few thousand. Next, IBM brought out the **XT**. Why XT? Possibly for eXTended Technology. Maybe because it was neXT. Beats me. Because the next one out was not called the YT but rather the **AT**. Probably that was for Advanced Technology. And then came a whole series called **PS/2**. All of these are micros sold by IBM.

Lots of smaller companies have produced machines that work just like the IBM micros. They are collectively called **Compatibles**, meaning compatible with IBM. Or IBM **Clones**.

To help define its capabilities, a micro might be referred to as a **286** or a **386** or a **486**. The AT is a 286 machine, which means that its main chip (the CPU) is an **Intel 80286** chip, or an imitation of it. A 386 is a machine based on the **80386** chip, etc. Each of these is roughly twice as powerful as the previous one. **Intel Corporation** is the company that created these chips: the 80286, 80386, 80486.

The latest, as of today, is the **Pentium**. The Intel Corporation decided enough was enough; no 586. There were all sorts of suggestions for a non-numeric name for the new 80586 chip, some clever and at least one rude. My favorite was "Big New Chip." But Pentium won out.

Will there be a 686? It won't be called that, but Intel is testing it as we speak. Intel is using **P6** as the program name for its 80686. No real name set yet. Some people thought it would be called Alpha, but **Digital Equipment Corp.** (usually called **DEC**) has preempted that. If you think of a good name for it, you should send it out to Intel. Considering they're using P6 right now, it sounds like they are in need of a good name. Information is that the P6 has 5.5 million devices engraved into its postage-stamp size. (The Pentium has a mere 3.1 million.)

Beyond the 686? They're working on it.

One interesting thing is that computer prices have not doubled when the speed doubled. No, not three times as much either. Generally, the price of the new (twice as powerful) machine is about the same as the price of the previous generation. So the now older-generation machine (although still manufactured and sold new) must go down in price to make room for the new one. Example: for *half* the cost of an XT (in 1984 dollars), today you can buy a machine 25 times faster, with sixteen times more memory, and 12 times more hard disk storage. Half as much money—and using 1994 dollars! Don't you wish they would do that on cars?

One note of caution. Be wary of offers on some cheap machines, "new" or otherwise. They may not be able to run some of today's new software.

... And a mouse

If a computer person thinks of an Apple as a machine, is it any wonder that he thinks of a **Mouse** as a device used to point to something on the computer screen (see monitor next chapter). Yes, that could be a finger. But computer people never do things simply. So they use a mouse. It's a small, fits-in-the-hand sized instrument with a ball barely sticking out of the bottom, and an electrical wire connecting it to the computer (makes a nice tail for the mouse). When the mouse is  moved around on the table top, or its own little rubber pad (appropriately called a **Mouse Pad**), the ball rolls, sending electrical signals to the computer which cause a little arrow on the screen to move in a similar fashion. Move the mouse right, the arrow goes right; move the mouse toward you, the arrow goes down.

The mouse has one, two or three buttons on the top, and when the person gets the arrow pointing at the right thing on the monitor screen, he pushes one of the buttons. If he pushes the correct button, something will happen that he wants to happen. As least, that's how it's supposed to work. If he pushes the wrong button, well ... . People refer to this operation as **point and click**. You use the mouse to move the arrow on the screen until it *points* at something you're interested in; then you enter that selection by pressing a button on the mouse and it makes a *"click"* sound.

That brings us to other pointing devices that in principle are the same as a mouse. The **trackball** is for people who don't like rodents. Here, the ball is simply mounted in a socket on the keyboard. You roll the ball in place and the arrow on the screen moves. These are often used on portables. (One wouldn't want to lose a mouse in the airport.) Then there's the **joystick**. I could let you guess, but I want to *stick* to the subject. It does the same thing, but uses just a small lever *stick*ing up, much like the old time steering devices on aeroplanes.

Two other approaches are the **light pen** and the **touch screen**. The light pen is like a mini-flashlight. You can use it to identify a particular spot on the screen. With the touch screen you *do* use your finger and touch the spot on the screen you want. You may have used these in museums or stores. But, you must have a special monitor (expensive) and the proper software. Even then, there are many tasks where the mouse is definitely superior to the finger. Sorry about that.

Throughout the remainder of the book, I'll *point* out some of the uses for these *point*ing devices.

Monitors, keyboards and terminals, oh my!

A **monitor**, sometimes called a **CRT** (which stands for Cathode Ray Tube), is like a small TV, without the commercials. It's connected to the computer and displays what the computer tells it to display. Hopefully, that matches what *you* want displayed. Sometimes the monitors are like black and white TV sets; sometimes they're in color.

As you are beginning to understand, computer techies are different from everyone else. So most of the one-color monitors (called **monochrome**) are not really black and white. They may be amber and black, or green and black. (Are you ready for this? There is often a price difference between amber, green and white. Does that make sense to you?) When the techies try to snow you with terms like **CGA, EGA, VGA**, etc., those are just different types of monitors. CGA is low resolution; EGA is medium resolution; and VGA is a newer version but still medium resolution.

The **keyboard** is the typewriter-like device for entering information. It has a standard typewriter keyboard, plus a bunch of other keys to make things easier, and is attached to the computer by an electric wire or cable to carry signals between the two. Some of the extra keys are called **function keys**, and are labeled **F1, F2**, etc. When one is pressed, it does a task it has been programmed to do. They just make things easier. Like, pressing F10 might automatically save your files to disk. You could save them without a function key; it's just easier with it.

A **terminal** includes both the monitor part and a keyboard. The keyboard may be **detached**, meaning it is connected to the monitor part by an electrical cord that looks a lot like a telephone cord. Older style terminals had the keyboard built in as part of the main chunk of terminal hardware. They were not as easy to maneuver to a comfortable typing position.

Peripherals

The disk drives, as well as the mice (if one had more than one mouse), trackballs and joysticks are all examples of what we call **peripherals**. In fact, just about everything that the computer doesn't absolutely *require* to run is a peripheral. Notice, I didn't say that you require. That's usually a lot more, particularly when someone really gets byten (oops, bitten) by the computer bug.

Technically speaking, the monitor and keyboard are peripherals. A microcomputer in your car gets along just fine without a monitor or keyboard. But if you and I want to use a computer, we'll have to have both.

Printers

So, a **printer** is a peripheral. And I won't insult you by telling you what a printer is. But there *are* different types so let's take a look at a few of them.

A **dot matrix** printer prints its numbers and letters by using lots of periods, or dots, ... Of course, it doesn't place all of them on the same line. It shapes them into letters or numbers. These are also called **serial**  printers because they print one character at a time. Quickly, of course. There are **line printers** that print an entire line at once, and **page printers** that print the entire page at once. Naturally, they cost more.

Then there are **ink-jet** printers. They use the same small dots as the dot matrix printers, but they make the dots by shooting  small drops of ink onto the paper. No, I am not kidding you; that's how they do it. And they do it very, very fast. Some print or draw in color, using several containers of ink and shooting out the right combination of colors to get the particular mauve or puce that you have asked for. They're not supposed to splatter.

As you know, there are also **laser printers** which work about like a photocopy machine. Since you don't see anything until the whole page pops out, they are Page Printers. And if the laser printer can print on both sides of the paper without you touching it, then it is a **duplex** printer.

Naturally, there are **color printers,** and you already know that doesn't mean they come in pretty cabinets. We mentioned that the ink-jet might be in color. A dot matrix could also be in color. There are also laser-like printers that are color printers. The typical laser printer only prints in one color. And while usually that means black, certainly it could be blue or brown by putting in a different **toner** (dry ink) cartridge. A red cartridge is almost impossible to find. And I've never seen puce. But there are newer (and more expensive) lasers that use several color toner cartridges simultaneously and by mixing the colors, they can print a page with many different colors. The good news is *you* don't have to do the color mixing.

Plotters draw pictures and are particularly good at maps, diagrams and large architectural drawings. Some plotters use a roll of paper, like a butcher does—or used to. So the plot could be fifty feet long, just in case you wanted to plot a map of a railroad line.

Can We Talk?

Modems allow a computer to send data across phone lines. I wouldn't bore you with the details, but someone in the back row did ask—modem is short for **MOdulate/DEModulate**.

 Roughly, this means changing the 0's and 1's the computer uses to sound waves the phone lines prefer, and then on the other end, changing the sound waves back to 0's and 1's. Hopefully, the end result matches what was sent. There are checking procedures which will usually let you know if the information received doesn't match the information sent.

A modem can be a board inside the computer or a separate box connected to the computer by a wire. In either case, it has to have a telephone line connected to it.

We all know about **fax** (or **facsimile**) machines. Well, of course many computer systems have a **fax board**—so the computer can send its own order to the pizzeria. As with modems, fax boards have built in phone jacks that must be connected to a phone line.

But what about *really* talking with the computer? We know that computers can talk to us; we've all gotten those annoying calls on the telephone where a computer talks to us instead of a person. With a good speaker, the computer can reproduce a voice extremely well. But can they listen?

Once more, computers imitate humans; computers can talk better than they can listen. With a microphone, the computer can pick up your voice. And it can record what it hears. And it can play it back to you. But it has real trouble understanding. However, they are improving. Before long, we may see the "conversational computer," much as in the movie "2001"—perhaps by the year 2001. Right now computers can read aloud to you, either from information stored on its disk or by scanning in printed text. Its pronunciation and voice quality is good and improving.

Today, some computers can recognize and respond to verbal commands using **Voice Recognition** software.. This is particularly helpful to some physically handicapped people, or persons whose hands are busy and cannot type in a command. If the system is trained for your voice, it can be quite accurate. This is particularly true for individual words.

It has much more difficulty with continuous speech.

However, considering all the work undertaken in the last 25 years, the results might seem unimpressive. But it is a very difficult problem. People living in the same town often have trouble understanding one another. Sometimes parents can't understand their own children. If we all had perfect diction, and expressed our thoughts clearly, the task would be easier and progress would be faster.

Computers are getting better all the time at understanding voice input. For certain, well-defined tasks, voice commands are actually being used with computers in the business world

 today. Some companies use voice recognition software to let computers take orders over the telephone. And the computer gets it right about as often as a person taking a message over the telephone—if that makes you feel any better.

What's the difference
between hardware and software?

Most of what we've talked about thus far is **hardware**: pieces of metal, plastic, wire, etc. Earlier, we defined what a program is. Well, a program is simply a piece of **software**. The Operating System mentioned earlier is software. A simple program that organizes your personal phone list is software. The complex program that calculates how to place a satellite into orbit is software. A collection of programs that an accounting firm might use to handle tax returns is software. And the program that runs Pac-Man or computer chess is software.

Software might come with the machine, or you might buy it in a store or through the mail, or you could write your own program. But they are all the same idea: a complete, often very complex, set of instructions which the computer will execute when requested to do so. To be a good program, the instructions must allow for no ambiguity; at each

step, there must be no confusion. If the program is accepting data being typed in at the keyboard, it must know what to do when a person hits two keys simultaneously or drops the phone on the keyboard. Or if a program is dividing numbers, it must know what to do if a divisor shows up as 0 (an illegal operation in mathematics). And even though a divisor should never be 0, you must tell the computer what to do if a 0 is offered as a divisor, because even if the computer doesn't make a mistake, a human might. And humans don't want their mistakes to cause a disaster.

Computer people all believe in Murphy's Law. A computer programmer needs to believe in Callan's law: If some situation should NEVER occur in a program, it probably will.

What happens if you don't take care of a situation and it pops up? There are two possibilities. The first is that the program will crash—maybe just the program, maybe the machine. That's the *good* news.

The second possibility is that the program will continue on. Why is that so bad, you ask? Because, since the programmer didn't tell the computer what to do, you have no idea what the computer *will* do. It might do something much worse than stopping. It could wipe out the last six months of work. It could write your data right in the middle of your boss's most important file. You don't know. And since the computer works so fast, it can, in the blink of an eye, trash the paper your boss is to read to a joint session of Congress. Better that your program crashes.

So, programs can be very simple, very complex, or anywhere in between. On very complex programs,—which many people may have worked on for years—there will always be places where every eventuality is not taken care of. Generally, these are situations that may never occur, or might not occur but once in two years. If it's in a game, or even a program to balance your checkbook, no big deal. If it is in a program controlling a Mars mission, it could be a billion dollar oversight.

Let's take just a couple of minutes to look at some of the most popular types of programs around today.

A **spread sheet** is a software program (of course, that's redundant, like saying high medical costs) which keeps information in rows and columns and is usually used in accounting applications. But not always. You could keep an address and phone list in a spread sheet. **1-2-3** from **Lotus Corp**. is one of the popular spread sheet programs for micros.

A **database** program keeps track of information that is related—any type of information. And it allows you to look at the information in any way (almost) that you want to, easily. For instance, you could look at a list of clients in alphabetical order, or by zip code, or area code, or by the type of orders they place, or by the frequency with which they place orders. You could select only records that meet some criteria you set. For instance, you could ask the computer to print a list of only those clients who spent over $100 with your firm in the last two months and who live in the zip code range you have chosen.

E-Mail allows for easy communication between people who have access to each other's computers, either through networks or via modems. (The E stands for electronic, not easy.)

Voice mail was designed to eliminate "telephone tag." That's when you call Joe, but he's not in and you leave your name and number. He calls while you're out. You call back but he's gone to lunch. He calls back ... Voice mail is like E-Mail with sound. You leave a message by talking (or singing or yelling) and not by typing. Both of these "mails" have some nice features not available with an ordinary answering machine. And both require a computer. Of course.

In a computer, an **editor** is not someone who looks over your work and cuts it to shreds. It's a program that allows you to enter information and make changes in it very easily.

A **word processor** is a program that aids in document preparation, like writing business letters or reports. It will include an editor and layout capabilities, and usually a  spelling checker, a thesaurus, maybe even a grammar checker. Some programs will show you on the screen exactly what the document will look like when printed out. This brings up everybody's favorite— **WYSIWYG—** pronounced wiz-ee-wig, which stands for **W**hat **Y**ou **S**ee **I**s **W**hat **Y**ou **G**et. That means, what you see on the monitor screen is exactly what it will look like on paper if you print it. If you don't have WYSIWYG, it probably won't. Some of the word processor products you may hear about are **WordPerfect, Microsoft Word**, and **Ami Pro**. There are many others.

A **Desk Top Publisher**, or **DTP**, goes beyond a word processor, getting into special type fonts, as well as leading and kerning and stuff you'd know about if you worked in the printing industry. In the end, the computer attempts to produce output worthy of a professional printer. Sometimes it does this very well. We go into more details in the chapter "Publish or Perish."

An **integrated software package** can do several of the individual things mentioned above (and/or some things not mentioned above). You might have a word processor and a spread sheet and graphics all in one package. Sort of a jack-of-all-trades.

Today, you also hear about **Suites**. A suite is a collection of programs which can work independently, or can pass data from one to another. Example: data from your spread sheet program is passed into your word processing program allowing you easily to put tables and graphs into a report, and produce better-looking output on your printer. Not a new concept, but a new marketing approach.

A **TSR** is a special kind of program. TSR stands for "**T**erminate and **S**tay **R**esident." It's sort of like our cat: nowhere in sight, but operate the can opener and he's right there. The TSR runs and then apparently goes away. But it's lurking in the background, and a single key stroke can immediately bring it up. It might even activate itself. It may be out of sight, but it is not out of the computer's mind or memory. Some examples of TSR's could be a calculator program that is residing in memory, though unseen, and pops up on the screen when you press some special key or combination of keys; or a program that watches in the background and when you do nothing for a long period of time, pops up and draws little fish swimming around on the screen. This is known as a screen-saver (see definition in the chapter "Tasty Leftovers"). Fax programs often have TSR's so the computer is ready to receive a fax, but can do other things until one comes along.

An important class of software is **compilers**. Remember, the computer understands only 0's and 1's. Someone had to write a translator so that the rest of us wouldn't have to think in 0's and 1's. So compilers take programs written in what is called a **high level language** (some closer to English than others) and translate them into a language that the computer can understand. A programming language, high level or low down, is simply a set of instructions a programmer can use to tell the computer (after a little help from the compiler) how to perform some task. **Basic** or **FORTRAN** or **COBOL** or **Lisp** or **C++** are examples of high level languages.

We'll talk about other types of programs later. But I don't want to choke you with too many at one time. They all sound like foreign languages.

Bugs and hackers

A **bug** is a mistake lurking in a program. Sometimes bugs may lie dormant for months or years, only to pop up and bring the program to a crashing halt. Maybe even the entire machine. Bugs have been known to take down a network. (For now, just think of a network as a number of computers connected together.) Because of the complex nature of some programs, there could be a bug in a program that would never show up; the particular set of circumstances which would trigger the bug just might not ever arise.

Bug is a polite word for "error." Computer programmers prefer "finding bugs" to "fixing errors."

A **programmer** is someone who writes programs for a computer. That means he or she writes exact instructions on how the computer is to accomplish a task.

Hackers

A **hacker** is a bit difficult to define. Like art. But a hacker is a computer programmer who is in love with his work—or hobby. In the computer world, hacker is not necessarily a denigrating term. It generally applies to someone who is not only good, but hard working. And usually someone who would rather work on the computer than climb the corporate ladder. Or a kid who would rather hack at the computer than play baseball.

Sometimes "hacker" is applied to a person who hacks—or intrudes—into a computer system or network where he has no business. Computer people sometimes refer to this type of hacker as a **cracker**. He might be doing it just to see if he can. Or he may be doing it to cause someone or some company trouble. Or he may be doing it for personal gain. For example, a student might try to hack into a school computer and change his grade. Or a criminal might try to breach a company's computer and alter accounts. In any event, it is "breaking and entering," and can result in criminal charges being filed against the intruder.

How does a cracker infiltrate a computer? Many computers have modems to allow persons to access information in the computer from a distance. For example, it is often helpful to a company for its salesmen to be able to call up the company computer and get information for a client, or some details about a prospective customer. Unfortunately, the cracker can

call the computer over the same public phone lines. It's up to the computer to control who gets in and who doesn't. Much work is being done in this area, but computer security systems are not perfect. Computers on networks (where many computers are able to communicate with one another) are particularly vulnerable; if someone can find a way into *one* of those, he may very well have access to all the computers on that network.

So, while it is desirable to be able to access the computer through a telephone line, it does present security problems. More on networks and security in a few pages.

Computer virus

Can computers get sick? They act like it some times. And I certainly have seen them die. And they definitely can get a virus.

Just as with humans, a computer gets a **Virus** from a "sick" person, someone who is mad at somebody or something or everything—or just mad. So he or she writes a very clever program. It hides on a computer and when the opportunity arises, it hops a ride to another computer. Without asking. Or telling. So it spreads, much like a virus.

A virus can be relatively harmless; it may just pop up every once in a while and say something nasty. You're sitting at the computer entering your Christmas card list and suddenly the screen goes black and in the middle of it is the message "Drop Dead, Creep." A more vicious virus might also wipe out your Christmas list. Or maybe wipe out half the information on your disk. Or trash the operating system.

But how does a virus get from one machine to another? Well, nowadays there is a great deal of communication between machines. Also, people pass information back and forth using diskettes. A virus can hide on a diskette and you

won't see it even if you print a list of files that are on that diskette. Remember modems? Computers talk to other computers over the phone lines. A virus can be transferred that way. Again, you won't see it. Then, there are public bulletin boards for computers (we haven't discussed those yet; but we will in a few pages). Most of these try to prevent any viruses from getting on them, but it is another possible way for a virus to spread.

A hermit isn't likely to get the Hong Kong flu. But those of us who are in contact with a lot of people are certainly at risk. The same thing is true for the computer. If it doesn't communicate with other computers, doesn't bring in any diskettes from outside or talk over the telephone lines, then it isn't likely to get a virus.

As with human viruses, there are many strains. (For the computer, that means many different virus programs that people have written.) Each one does something different. But they are all bad, whether unpleasant or deadly.

Is there any good news? Yes. Humans can't catch a virus from a computer, no matter how robot-like a computer person might seem. (I must admit, though, I have seen several people get really sick when they discovered a virus had attacked their computer.) And while a virus may erase or garble files or directories, it won't really damage the hardware.

Just like in humans, you can **inoculate** your computer against viruses.

Hold it right there, you say. Do you give the computer a shot, or a pill twice a day? Just how do you inoculate a computer? Actually, you put on a special program, an **Antivirus program**, that watches to see if certain viruses try to transfer themselves on to your machine. It prevents them from moving in, or evicts them  if they are already there. You can think of the antivirus program as the computer's *board*er patrol.

Unfortunately the analogy continues: you vaccinate against specific viruses, so another type or strain of virus can still infect the computer.

But, no pills. No shots.

Can a computer think?
If so, what does it think about?

Every time we get into a discussion of thinking, it turns out to be thought-provoking. What does it mean to think? Does a flower think? How does it know when to bloom or when to close its petals for the night.

If we say that the flower does not think, but simply reacts to certain stimuli around it, then a computer does not think. It follows instructions. Although people who use computers sometimes doubt this, the computer does not go off and think up ways to be difficult. It is not a Dennis the Menace. It follows to the letter the instructions it receives. If a situation arises for which it has no directive, that's a horse of a different color. There's no telling what it will do.

But does it think? With astute programming, the computer can access various pieces of information in its memory and use this to produce answers in such a way that it appears to be thinking. Example: it has been given addition and multiplication tables, so when we ask it to add, subtract, multiply, etc. it will do that. However, it is not thinking; it is simply following the instructions we gave it. Of course, when we teach our children the addition and multiplication tables and then they add and multiply numbers, we say how smart they are.

Example: we tell the computer all about the symptoms of a certain illness. We give it even more information on backgrounds and circumstances that might lead to this illness. In fact, we try to tell it everything that a good doctor might know about this illness. This information is stored in its permanent memory (disk). Then, in walks a patient. As we find out about the patient—temperature, symptoms, medical history—we input that into the computer. While the computer cannot push on a muscle and ask if it hurts, the doctor pushes and asks, then gives the answers to the computer. It gets all the information that the doctor gets. Utilizing the data it already has in its permanent memory, and following the rules that have been programmed into it, the computer will match the information on this patient and make a diagnosis. If it's the right program and the right illness, the computer may make as good a diagnosis as the doctor. Maybe even better, because it won't be tired and forget something. Or maybe worse, because it doesn't have a sixth sense, or a gut feeling. It's very hard to program gut feelings or a sixth sense, (or compassion, for that matter) into a computer.

Did the computer think when it made the diagnosis? Probably it was not thinking, but following instructions. But, did the computer show intelligence? Many would say yes. It did something that, if a human did it, we would say it was intelligent. But didn't we have to put all the information into the computer and tell it how to use it? Yes. But then, medical school probably did much the same for the doctor.

The type of program described above is called an **Expert System**, so named because the programmer tries to capture the knowledge and experience of an "expert" and use that to drive a computer program. Expert systems are part of the larger area of computer work known as **Artificial Intelligence,** or **AI** as it is often called,

Of course, humans can extend their knowledge. They can learn, decode, infer, leap, realize, conclude and move on to totally different areas of knowledge. Some AI programs help the computer do similar things. It can devise new rules. If it gets feedback (just as we humans need) it can improve, learning what works and what does not. To many, this is a clear indication of an intelligent program, or an intelligent computer.

One thing is certain. (I think.) A computer can produce answers that you would call intelligent, if they were given to you without you knowing where they came from. This is a test that is often applied to AI programs. If you didn't know it came from a machine, would you call it intelligent?

Some other names you may hear that describe different approaches to artificial intelligence, are **Knowledge Based Systems**, **Heuristic Systems**, **Machine Learning**, **Robotics**, **Natural Language** and **Voice Recognition**.

If a computer does think, what does it think about? Only what someone has programmed it to deal with. AI work has progressed in many area, including but not limited to: games, vehicle routing, medical diagnosis, investment analysis, financial planning, insurance planning, mining, design problems of many types, machine repair, contract bidding, instruction, and others.

While an AI system may expand its ability in a field, it won't switch fields. If the program deals with finding oil, it won't have a mid-life crisis and decide to be a doctor. It might suggest a new approach to determining geological structures for an oil company, but it won't tell you that your allergy is actually a vitamin deficiency.

Will the computer balance my checkbook?

Yes.

Well, it's not that simple. But I thought for once I'd give a one-word answer.

There are programs that will allow you to input your checks and deposits, interest earned and fees charged and then balance everything for you. If you don't make a mistake on the input, the computer will not make a mistake on the balance.

But if you forget a check or a fee or a deposit, (I never forget a deposit) then the computer can't give you the right balance.

Some of the programs will also write checks for you. For instance, if you have a monthly payment that is always the same, you simply ask for that check and—if you have checks that work in your computer printer—the computer will print it out for you with today's date. Unhappily, it won't stuff it in an envelope for you and it won't provide a stamp. (Are you

like me? Anybody who sends me a postage-paid return envelope always gets paid first.) Bills that you owe every month, but for different amounts—say, the electric bill or the telephone bill—can be organized so that you simply put in the new amount. The computer handles the rest, including recording the amount in the computer's check register.

Some programs will print various reports for you. For instance, you can get a check register, or a list of all payments to credit cards, or a list of all tax-deductible payments, or a total of all beauty shop expenses, or the total spent at the grocery store, or the cost to have the parakeet groomed. And of course, a balance sheet.

It will search for a check or deposit based on the payee, the date, or the amount. And it will find it instantly—well, very rapidly. It will balance your account against the bank statement and tell you which checks have not cleared, etc.

The choices for handling household expenses are wide. You can find one that has the amount of detail that is right for you. Unfortunately, none will provide the money to cover those checks.

Isn't it nice to know there's still a place for the human after all?

Are there potholes on the information highway?

C omputer people love networks. And that has nothing to do with NBC, CBS, ABC, FOX, or CNN. Computer **networks** allow computers to talk to one another, and people on different computers to talk to one another. It's the electronic age version of the old party line. You pick up the phone, see who's talking, and join in if you wish.

There is a real danger here. Suppose computers find just how much they know and take control of the business world? I've seen movies where the computer goes berserk. Sometimes I think we work for the computers already.

Nevertheless, since it's a lot of trouble to carry a disk full of data from one computer to another, and slow, too, (particularly if they're 82 miles apart), we hook computers up where data can be shared between various computers and peripherals. And people too. So a person on computer A might get some information from a file on computer B and print out a report on a printer that is attached to computer C. Computers A, B and C might be in the same building or in different states. Example: I'm sitting at my computer in Dallas. I get some information over the network from a company computer in Houston, prepare a report on Texas sales and print it out on the sales manager's printer in Chicago—if the people in Chicago left any paper in the printer. If the computers are all connected to one company wide network, I might not even need to know what cities they're in.

What kind of things get hooked into the network? Could be computers, printers, terminals, modems, or anything that communicates with computers. Each of these would be called a **Node** on the network.

A **LAN** is a **L**ocal **A**rea **N**etwork. Nothing tricky here. This means the things hooked to the network are "local", or somewhat close. Think of it as in one building, or on one campus.

Suppose the law school in the suburbs has its computers attached to a LAN; let's call it LAWLAN. Downtown, the business school of that university has its computers connected on a LAN, the BUSINET. It would be nice if someone on LAWLAN could communicate with someone on BUSINET. A **bridge**, or a **gateway**, can connect the two networks. A **router** helps the computers deliver info to the right person, regardless of which network the person is on.

There are, of course, different types of LAN's. **Ethernet** and **token rings** are just two types of lans whose names you may hear. They handle the traffic (data) differently.

A **Wide Area Network**, or WAN, can cover, by means of telephone lines, dedicated lines, microwave signals, satellites, etc., as wide an area as you need.

Internet is a large network connecting many other networks. Every computer on each of those networks, tens of thousands of computers actually, all over the U.S. and many foreign countries, has access to all the others, to some extent. Right now, this is about as close as we are to the **Electronic Highway** or **Information Super Highway** that people talk about. Today, access is limited, although not as much as you might expect. Millions of people use it and abuse it already.

Are there any pot holes on this superhighway? Of course there are! And like all roads, the worst pot holes are the ones we don't see. There'll be datajackings (people stealing your

data); collisions, resulting in crashed computers, smashed data and lost information; and bridges out when your data must get through. The first law suit over messages posted on the Internet has already been filed. $200 million asked.

And it *will* be a toll road.

What good is an Information Super Highway to me? And where's the entrance ramp—just in case I want to go for a Sunday drive? (Or "**surf the net**," as they say these days.)

For most people, the easiest way to get on the infoway is through a commercial network, such as **America On Line, Compuserve, Delphi, GEnie, Prodigy**, etc. There are local phone numbers in most cities of any size, say 50,000 or more.

Once you're on the network, you can—from your personal computer at home — access an unbelievable array of information: reference works, library catalogs, stock market information, newspapers. You can make your own airline or hotel reservations, look at research projects from hundreds of universities, get reviews of movies and books, exchange ideas or recipes with strangers who live thousands of miles away, check the going price for your car or that old baseball card you found in the attic, get the weather forecast for a city you're flying to tomorrow, or find out when and where the next "Star Trek" convention is. It is this unparalleled access to information that gives rise to names such as **Iways**, highways for information, or the **Infopike**, as *Variety* calls it.

This ability to move and probe in all directions made another descriptive name for such networks inevitable: **Cyberspace**. Sound like science fiction? It's not. It's fact.

It is possible—actually easy—to display on your computer's monitor in your home an old civil war picture that resides in the Library of Congress. And enlarge a portion of it so you can look more closely at some of the details. If you've done this before (so you know how to go about it), the process should take only a few minutes. And you can do this while you're sitting snowbound in Casper, WY.

The **World Wide Web**, or simply **WWW**, is a facility, or sub-culture, on the Internet which links documents, graphics, sound and video to related information, some of which could be stored in distant locations. Generally, just by using the mouse to point to a word and pressing a button, additional information, graphics, etc. related to the selected word will be brought to your screen. For instance, the home page for the "Lois and Clark" TV show lists all its publicity photos. You just select those you want and down-load them to your computer, then print them on your laser printer.

There are speed bumps. Downloading some files can take 5, 10, 20 minutes. Of course, it might save you hours or days.

With so much information, how do you ever find anything? Programs such as **InfoSeek**, **Yahoo, Lycos** and others do much of the searching for you. You give it key words, it searches thousands of computers and offers possible matches. Work in this area, **Information Retrieval**, or **IR**, is moving fast. InfoSeek is said to handle over 300,000 queries/day already. Programs which help you navigate the Web are called **Web Crawlers** or, logically, **Spiders**.

Not all services are available through all nodes, and some make it easier than others. But the technology is in use today, by both paeans and professors. And the information super highway is already carrying a lot of traffic.

Like all highways, this one will need a highway patrol. The possibilities for crime here are far greater than on any street. White collar crime, theft, smuggling, terrorism and child pornography are very real threats. (The National Center for Missing and Exploited Children has a pamphlet entitled "Child Safety on the Information Highway.") And as the use of **digital cash** or **E-cash**, expands (it's already being used)—allowing shopping and paying in cyberspace without using credit cards—so will crime. Cyber fraud is evident now.

Before we leave networks, let's look at the local variety again. Two approaches to LANs that you might hear people mention are client/server and peer-to-peer networks.

Client/server networks use a central computer that oversees the network and provides storage for most files used on the network. It's the server. All other computers are the clients.

A **file server**, sometimes called a **network server**, is a

"Your file, Sir."

special computer on the network where users can store files, gain access to files shared by others, etc. Generally, a file server is characterized by a fast machine and large disks designed to make each user feel like he is the *only* user.

Not always achieved.

In **peer-to-peer** networks, each computer is equal—at least philosophically. (You know down deep that yours is better than Joan's. And George is sure that everybody's is better than his.) Each can access files on the other computers, but no one is really a "server" to the others. Of course, you can choose to protect some, or all, of your files as private and therefore not accessible by others.

One of the earlier networks created at M.I.T. about 20 years ago was called **CHAOS**. Perhaps its creators could see the future of networks.

If a computer designs a bridge, who's responsible if it falls down?

This is a complex problem. Let's break it down and see what we can see.

Currently, a person is designated as the architect, or structural engineer, for the bridge. He, or she, is responsible

for its design. He may use a computer; today, that is almost a certainty. The computer will simply follow instructions. So if it presents erroneous data, there are three possibilities. First, the person running the computer entered the wrong data on which the calculations were based. He input "20 cars" when he meant to type "200 cars". Left off a 0. Now the load calculations are based on only 1/10 the weight they should be. That's the most likely possibility and we know exactly where to place the blame—if we are looking for somewhere to place the blame.

Second, the program that makes the calculations could be wrong. Maybe the programmer put in, for example, A plus B, when it should have been A times B. Clearly, the programmer made a mistake. But then, no structural engineer worth his hard hat would use a program for an important job that he had not checked very carefully. He would run tests, knowing the answer, and make sure that the computer agreed. In all likelihood, he'd run a different program to check the first program.

Third, there could have been an undetected hardware failure. This is not very likely. There may have been a failure, but failures are usually obvious. But not always. An error in the Pentium chip went undetected for a long time.

So, it's pretty clear that the structural engineer carries the load on his shoulders. Today, at least.

The present mind-set is to have some human really in charge, but as the use of artificial intelligence programs expand, who knows what will happen.

Let's explore this a bit. The cold war is over and we're not so concerned about attack and counter attack as we were two decades ago. But in the future, things will move at an even faster pace. Will they be moving too fast for humans to react? Will we find ourselves *needing* the computer to make a decision, to start something in motion in order to save time and lives? If the "star wars" defense system were actually implemented, with bullets shooting bullets, would we require computers to decide, in a time period too short for humans to react, when and where to fire a satellite-killing laser beam? Do we trust the computer with that kind of decision?

I believe the computer will follow instructions exactly. With redundant systems, I believe they will be reliable. But with millions of instructions, could there be a situation not covered? Could there be a glitch?

Yes. Not every possibility could be tested. As the computer systems become more sophisticated, could the computer put its own safety first? It could be programmed to protect the most valuable assets first. An intelligent computer might determine that since it made very important decisions, its own safety should come before that of humans. Scary stuff. And not out of the question at all.

That's one reason why, ultimately, we hold humans responsible.

Doctors don't use expert systems much today. Why not? As a rule, they don't understand how the computer arrives at its conclusions. And since they are responsible for their patients, they don't want to accept a decision without knowing precisely where it came from. That will change someday, but not any time soon.

Parlez vous Pascal?

A s we mentioned in the Chapter "Bits and Bytes," computers basically have a very limited vocabulary. 0 and 1. (Sometimes kids think that's the size of their parents' vocabulary: "no" and "later.")

The first applications were programmed using long strings of 0's and 1's, but that got tiresome in a hurry. And it was certainly error prone. If the mother of invention is necessity, the father is laziness. So, new "languages" were developed to make life a little easier.

Much of the first computer work was on scientific and engineering problems. So in the early 1950's, the first "high level" computer language was developed. It was called **FORTRAN,** from **FOR**mula **TRAN**slator. IBM gets a lot of the credit here. FORTRAN allows the scientist or programmer to write instructions for the computer in a form more natural to mathematicians and engineers. FORTRAN has been improved over the years, allowing for much more than scientific programming, but it is still widely used for mathematical programming.

By 1960 **COBOL** (**CO**mmon **B**usiness **O**riented **L**anguage) was on the scene. During the sixties, there were such languages as SNOBOL, MAD, SAD, GOTRAN, etc. as many universities created their own computer language. Talk about a Tower of Babel! The computer community had its own.

You hear people mention **BASIC**. Just what is it? It stands for **B**eginners **A**ll purpose **S**ymbolic **I**nstruction **C**ode. It was developed at Dartmouth College in the mid 60's. It started as a simple language for beginners on mainframe machines. It was later moved to minicomputers. And then on to PC's. It is an easy and fast way to get started in programming—and you can do a lot with it.

PASCAL was developed around 1970. Several later languages used it as a model, notably **Ada**, commissioned by the Department of Defense, which decreed that all of its programs would be written in one language: Ada. Anyone wanna bet on that?

C, C+ and **C++** could be considered mixed breeds: they are high level languages, but they allow the programmer to manipulate the machine at a reasonably low level. Sort of the best of both worlds (or the worst, depending on your point of view). They are good for developing other software. For example, a computer operating system named **UNIX** was written in the C language.

dBASE had a noble beginning. It was originally written to keep track of a company football pool, or so the story goes. It became the first relational data base program for the emerging microcomputers around 1980, even before IBM decided to stick its toe in the water. There are now a number of **Data Base Management System** (**DBMS**) programs including **Paradox** and **FoxPro**. There had been, of course, DBMS programs on mainframes much earlier.

When someone says **OOPS**, you tend to look and see what he dropped. But if it's a computer nerd, he may well be talking about an **O**bject **O**riented **P**rogramming **S**ystem. The object-oriented approach is very flexible, yet very powerful. An early OOPS was **SMALLTALK** from Xerox. It was used to produce one of the very first GUI's (see the next chapter).

LISP (**LIS**t Processing) also dates back to about 1960. It is a high level language for non-numeric programming. (It can do numbers, but that is not its forte.) It is the language of choice for many Artificial Intelligence programmers.

So, why all these languages? Wouldn't we all be better off speaking the same thing? Maybe English?

Just as the French and Russians wouldn't agree that English is best, neither will programmers agree to just one language.

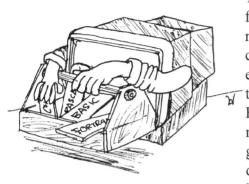

There are dozens of fields of work that need (want?) a computer language especially suited for their type of problems. FORTRAN is best for math; COBOL is geared for business. dBASE handles data bases well; LISP makes for more productive AI people. C++ makes the tough work of writing computer games ... well, if not fun, at least easier.

As with any craft, there are a variety of tools that look similar to the layman. To the craftsman, these tools are different and each one has a job it's best suited for.

So there remains work for computer language developers. Keeps them off the streets.

Gooey Windows in Chicago

his might have something to do with a hole-in-the-wall cafe, but you know better, don't you? This is about computers. A **window** is an area of the computer monitor's screen in which something different from the rest of the screen can be happening. (Like the "picture in a picture" on some new TVs.)

You could have several windows, all with different things happening. (Well, of course. Wouldn't it be silly to have the *same* thing going on in all of them!) Windows are very useful and are found in many applications.

But now, things get a little sticky. Microsoft Corporation, the software giant, has built a **user interface** (the part of a computer program that the person—user—sees and uses) called **"Windows"**. So when someone says he or she is using windows, you have to ask "Is that with a capital W?"

"Windows" is one of the best-selling pieces of software on the market right now, so it's likely that when people talk about Windows, they mean capital W—from Microsoft. If they talk about a window, that's probably small w.

"Windows" is a **G**raphical **U**ser **I**nterface, or **GUI** (pronounced gooey) for short. A GUI uses pictures rather than words whenever possible, and allows the user to point (using a mouse—remember him?) rather than type.

An **Icon** is a little picture on the screen to help those who have trouble with words. For instance, suppose you wanted to get rid of a file—delete it. If you forget the word for delete, you might see a picture of a trash can and realize that you want to "throw the file away". So you use the mouse to position the little white arrow on the screen over the name of the file to be trashed. Then by pushing the right button (actually, it's usually the left button that is right), you grab the file name, move it over and deposit it in the trash. Obviously, you need some sort of pointing device (mouse, trackball, etc.) to use icons. Not all systems use icons, but the "G" in GUI does stand for Graphical and indicates that GUI systems depend on icons.

Personally, I view these like "universal symbols" they put on things. My lawn mower has pictures of a turtle and a rabbit (I guess they're really a tortoise and a hare) for slow and fast—I think. But I'm not sure. Since the tortoise won the race, maybe the tortoise is for fast and the hare for slow. A picture may be worth a thousand words, but if I only need one or two words, I'd prefer the words.

However, "Windows" was designed specifically to make the computer easier to use, working for a "**User Friendly**" system: non-intimidating and easy to use. Once you get adept at using a mouse, you can be quite productive with Windows.

If you hear a computer person talking about Chicago, there's a good chance he is referring to a new release of Windows called **Chicago**.   When released, it will likely be called **Windows 95**. **Windows for Workgroups** is a Peer-to-Peer Network using Windows.   (These are all capital W's— Microsoft.)

A **menu** is simply a list of items to choose from, generally in a little box, or window (small w) on the screen.   Just like a ... menu. **Pop-up menus** are sub-menus that suddenly appear on the screen sometimes when you choose an item on one menu that gives you even more choices.   It's like the main menu in a restaurant listing an item that says "Desert Menu Available".   You choose deserts and immediately the waiter hands you a desert menu with many specific choices. **Pull down menus** - same thing. You can have sub-menus of sub-menus, or pop-ups that come from pull downs. Basically, they are simply windows on the screen that provide choices or information.

And with that, we'll close the curtains on this window.

Multimedia—a window to the future

One of the hot topics in the computer community right now is multimedia. Nothing tricky here, for a change. **Multimedia** means combining several media. In reality, you only combine two: audio and visual. But it sounds more impressive if you say you're combining different kinds of visual and audio media. So multimedia combines text, audio, graphics, animated graphics and full-motion video, etc. That allows computer presentations to  appeal to (or offend) more of your senses than could be done with mono-media, a single medium.

With the right equipment you can program your microcomputer to make a presentation like a TV. You need a very fast computer and one with lots of memory (RAM) and lots of hard disk storage. And you'll need a **Sound Board** (one popular brand is called **Sound Blaster**) into which you can plug very good speakers, capable of blasting the ears off older people. You can play CD's and, using a microphone, record music or voice to the hard disk.

You could put on a **MIDI** (which stands for **M**usical **I**nstrument **D**igital **I**nterface). With one, you can plug in a MIDI compatible synthesizer, for instance. Now you have an incredible tool for a composer! For example, you can set the

synthesizer to guitar and play the lead on the keyboard. The computer will recognize (through the MIDI) the notes you play, the length of each, tempo, etc. and write the sheet music for you. You can then set your keyboard for a bass, have the computer play back the lead guitar part, and you join in and play bass. The computer adds a staff and writes the music for the bass. Then do the same thing for the drums. You can do as many parts as you want to. When you finish, you can have the computer play all the parts together, and then print out the music for each instrument.

Suppose you decide your composition should be written in D major instead of B minor. You simply ask the computer to transpose it for you. It can do that about as fast as you can read this sentence. You want a different tempo? Just ask for it. Want to add lyrics? The computer will display the music and you type the words where you want them. And of course changes can be made with very little trouble..

You may hear **MPC** mentioned. That's short for **Multimedia PC**, which means a PC that is big enough and fast enough to handle multimedia. Microsoft and others have determined a set of minimums (memory, speed, disk space, etc.) that a computer should have to effectively use multimedia. A computer must meet these requirements to be designated MPC.

Clearly, this is the face of the future. No longer will the monitor display a message saying that with its current settings, it can't find the file you have requested. Rather, it will say in a pleasant voice that with its current settings, it can't find the file you have requested. Or it might show a picture of a person wearing a dunce hat and blast through its speakers "Hey, dummy, did you spell the name correctly?"

Moving just a little bit further, some of these problems may be solved as you simply say the name of the file you want to retrieve. This is available today, to a limited extent.

A very interesting item, available now—but too expensive for individual use—is **video conferencing**. Until now, it has required a great deal of equipment and someone with at least a masters degree in electrical engineering to set it up. Big bucks. However, that is about to change. A small, inexpensive camera can be attached to your computer and with the proper software, you can talk with someone (who has a similar setup) and at the same time have a video image of him or her on  your computer monitor. In fact, that live, real-time picture could occupy just a portion of your screen, while the document or drawing you are discussing fills the rest of the screen. So you and the person in Poughkeepsie can make changes in the document; you can each see the changes as they are happening. And you can see the look on his face when you correct his spelling.

Of course, this would also work on a computer network. It doesn't have to be across a telephone line.

Probably by the time you read this, such a system can be yours for maybe 4,000 smackers. By the time you actually decide to buy one, the price will have dropped to half that. Today, video conferencing is rare. In five years, it will be—well, common place may be a bit overstated—widely used.

There's a mouse on my toaster

The name might throw you, but a **video toaster** is really a microcomputer with special software.

Perhaps the easiest way to explain a video toaster (or simply **toaster**, as most users would call them) is to tell you what you can do with it. You could produce all the fancy displays that you see in commercials on TV. Signs that swoop down, turn over and around and then fade off into the sunset. Words that shake, shimmy, change size and color, stretch, grow wheels and drive off. Tigers that morph into kittens, or people that morph into green monsters or lions. And you can add in actual video clips that you recorded with your home video camera.

Why is it called a toaster? The story is that the original creator said he wanted it to be as easy to use as a toaster.

It *is* pretty neat—but it is *not* as easy to use as a toaster.

Still, for 5,000 bucks and a lot of work, you could produce commercials like the big agencies do with $100,000 equipment. You could even make your own Bud Bowl.

Some of the special effects in adventure movies are produced, at least partially, on a toaster.

So, if someone says they got a mouse to put on their toaster, don't faint. A mouse or joystick is a very useful thing to have on any multimedia PC, including a video toaster.

One of the things a mouse lets you do in these graphic gyrations is "**drag and drop**". That means you can identify some area or item on the screen (by using the mouse to position the screen arrow over that item) and select it by pressing down the left button on the mouse. Then, while holding the button down, you move the mouse which drags the item selected across the screen and then deposit (drop) it at a new location by releasing the button. Sort of like having a teenager too young to drive.

Pick a card, any card

In the second chapter, we talked about the motherboard. In most microcom-puters, there are other **boards,** also called **Cards**, and they plug into a socket on the motherboard. Like the motherboard, they are printed circuit boards, that is, they have electrical circuits printed, or molded, onto the board. They will also have a variety of electronic compo-nents attached to them

That brings us to **expansion slots**. Those could be extra slot machines at the casino in case additional customers come in. Or they could be the sockets on the motherboard into which you can plug computer cards. Take a guess; you've got a 50-50 chance on this one, certainly better than you get on the slot machines.

So what good are the cards since they're too clumsy to play games with?

Controller cards, sometimes called **interface cards,** allow the computer to deal with things attached to the computer (peripherals). For instance, there is a **disk controller**, so that the computer can deal with disks. The **printer controller** is the link between the computer and the printer. And so on. Sometimes they are called **adapters**, such as a **display adapter** which is the go-between for the computer and a display. Some cards can handle several of these tasks.

There are **memory cards**. They won't help *your* memory, even if you stick one in your pocket. But they do allow you to add on more memory (RAM) than will fit on the motherboard directly. Older computers needed a large board for 1 megabyte of memory. Today, 4, 8 or 16 megs (depending on the memory chip used) can fit on a tiny memory card. Many new computers can use 64 or even 256 megabytes of memory. However, even as memory gets cheaper, few non-business micros warrant the cost of even 128 megabytes. Today, that might be $5,500 just for the memory.

Network cards allow the computer to hook up to a network. A **modem card** is the middle man between the phone line and the computer. And a **sound board** is a card that will drive speakers (see multimedia).

As you can see, "cards" and "boards" are used pretty much interchangeably.

If we have a motherboard, it seems reasonable to have a **daughter board**. These are smaller boards that plug into another board, not into the motherboard as a rule. We skip a generation, so to speak. Seems like it should be a granddaughter board.

Interface software or **driver software** makes the various parts work together. So the actual interface between two things (the two things could be you and the computer, even) generally consists of both hardware and software.

Cards can be as cheap as $15, for a simple printer interface in a microcomputer, for instance. In a mainframe computer, a controller may be several cards, or an entire cabinet full. Plus the software. And might cost as much as a car.

The disk controller card plugs into the motherboard, but not the disk. So there are cables that run from the controller board to the disk drive, generally all inside the cabinet on a micro. On the other hand, the controller card for a printer has a socket that sticks out the back of the computer cabinet and you plug a cable from the printer into that socket. The same thing is true for the keyboard. A small wire runs from the keyboard and plugs into a socket on the back of the computer cabinet. For a modem card, it's a phone line you plug in.

There are a number of sockets on the back of the computer cabinet. Each type has its own unique size or shape. So, when you start to plug something into the computer, the chances are there is only one socket that will fit. For example, the keyboard has a round plug. On the back of the computer, there is only one round socket of the correct size.

Proceed to the next chapter for more on the exciting world of interconnections.

Any port in a storm

If a sea port is a way to get in and out of a country, then it surely follows that a computer **port** is a way to get into, or out of, a computer. And it is.

A **printer port** is the physical place the printer interfaces with the computer. A **com port**, short for **communications port**, is used for various forms of communication in and out of a computer, for example, a modem, and a mouse.

Ports are divided into two main types: Serial and Parallel. The **serial port** passes information serially, that is, one bit at a time. Sort of like a procession of ants. Since a bit is either a 0 or a 1, it takes about eight bits to send a character. With postage and handling, it ends up being more like 10 bits. So, at 1,200 **BPS** (bits per second) that amounts to 120 letters per second. At an average of 6 characters per word (and the space between words takes just as much time to send as a W),

Serial

that's only about 20 words per second. Sure sounds a lot faster if you say 1,200 BPS. **Baud** is roughly equivalent to BPS; 9600 Baud = 9600 BPS (about 160 words per second).

A **parallel port** sends more than one bit at a time. It uses a bunch of wires on its plug so it can send an entire byte, or more, at once. Right off, you can tell it's going to be faster. No single-file ants, here; more like soldiers ants on parade.

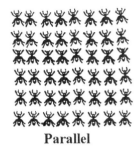

Parallel

O.K., but what are these things *physically*? Basically, ports are sockets found on the back of the computer. They could be part of a card in the computer, or they could be attached directly to the motherboard. They can be round (the keyboard plug fits into the round socket), or D shaped, or a telephone type socket to connect the modem to the phone line. The D shaped plugs can be several sizes and have different looks, depending on the number of wires they are prepared to handle and the particular technology used.

Unfortunately, you can't use any port in a storm. You either use the designated one, or you sink.

Chips and dips

In the chapter "The inside story", we mentioned IC's and promised to talk a little bit about them later. This is later; let's talk.

An **integrated circuit**, or **IC** or **chip**, is a lot of electronic circuits put on one small piece of **silicon**. (The area between San Francisco and San Jose is called **Silicon Valley** because

of the number of companies there engaged in producing or using IC's.) IC production starts with silicon in the form of common sand or quartz,

Back to it roots

refines it to large, ultra-pure crystals, and proceeds through as many as 200 steps to produce the final chip. I won't cover all of those today, but I will say that much of it is carried out in an environment 1,000 times cleaner than a hospital operating room.

Literally millions of tiny circuits, or devices, can be etched onto a silicon chip the size of your little fingernail. Saves a lot of space. The Pentium chip with 3.1 million circuits takes about as much room as three transistors did 35 years ago. That's why that little notebook computer is actually more powerful than the room-sized monsters of thirty years ago. And faster too. (Not the biggies of today, of course.)

IC's are sort of like engraving the Lord's prayer on the head of a pin. Only now, it's the entire New Testament. Tomorrow, maybe the whole Bible. You're going to need eyes *better* than a teenager's. Fortunately, the computer will read it and then print it out in somewhat larger type for us. Incidentally, there are computers that will print your material in Braille, or use a speaker and read it out loud.

Another reason that the IC has had such an impact on computers is their power consumption. IC's use a lot less electricity than the vacuum tubes of old or even the early IC's that had five circuits on a chip. That also means they generate a lot less heat. Today's micros don't require special electrical circuits or air conditioning.

Semiconductors are not apprentice conductors. They're more like part-time, or guest, conductors. A Semiconductor is a device that conducts current only when some traffic cop (in the computer) says go. And believe it or not, that is the essence of today's computers—tens of thousands or millions of semiconductors engraved onto a tiny IC. People speak of transistors as an important break through for the computer industry some 40 years ago. A **Transistor** is a type of a semiconductor.

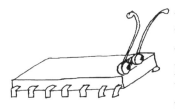

As we've noted, these IC's are quite small and subject to damage. So they get packaged in plastic, with the connecting wires sticking out. Some of them are **DIP's**, which stands for Dual In-line Package. That means the wires connected to the chip stick out of the plastic package on both of the long sides. The effect is to produce a bug looking thing, which can be plugged into a socket on a computer board, or soldered in place. A **SIP** is a chip in a Single In-line Package—only one row of legs, like a bug that lost all its left feet.

On the memory side, we have **SIMM's**, or Single In-line Memory Modules. These are actually small computer cards, about 3 inches long and maybe a half inch wide. They can contain, depending on the type of chips put on them, from 1 megabyte of memory to 16 megabytes of memory. Remember, each byte is 8 bits. So that small card that holds 16 megabytes of memory, contains 128 million bits—all on a tiny card with a total size of 1 ½ square inches. Incredible!

Publish or perish

Back in the chapter on Hardware and Software, we mentioned Desk Top Publishing. And somewhere else we talked about laser printers. Let's put those together, along with a few other things.

With the improved formatting and graphic capabilities on computers, and the increased resolution (quality of print) on the laser printers, it is now possible to produce high-quality output on a microcomputer system.

A good **Desk Top Publishing (DTP)** system allows for the integration of text, graphics (such as logos, cartoons or photographs which can be scanned into the computer from outside pictures, or created internally), borders, automatic pagination, page and chapter numbering and precise typographic alignment. With WYSIWYG (what you see is what you get) you can rapidly preview before you print.

To scan in pictures, an **optical reader**, or **scanner**, is passed over the picture. It converts the picture into a series of dots (these may be color or black and white). This is called **digitizing**. The result is a digital representation of the picture. The quality depends on how fine the sampling is (how many dots per inch in each direction). A newspaper picture is generally only about 85 dots per inch. Fairly inexpensive computer **scanners** can handle 400 dots per inch.

The resolution on a monitor screen is roughly 100 dots per inch. Each dot on the screen is called a **pixel**. I like the sound of that. Like pixie. But the computer is unromantic. To it, a pixel is a single dot. Worse yet, it is short for **Picture Element**. They didn't even get all the letters right!

On the output side, modern laser printers can produce images with resolutions from 300 to 1800 dots per inch. This is sufficient for all but the most exacting work. Just think, at 600 dots per inch, you have 360,000 dots in one square inch. Going to 1,200 dots per inch means nearly a million and a half dots in one square inch. Good resolution.

> 1 square. inch

With this high resolution, laser printers can produce a wide variety of fonts. A **Font** is a collection of letters and symbols in a particular type face, style, size and weight. The main text of this book is a Times New Roman (**type face**), upright (**style**), 12 point (**size**), regular (**weight**). But we could change from upright to *Italics*. Or we could change from regular to **Boldface**. We could switch from 12 point to 16 point. Or we might decide to trade in the Times New Roman and print in the OzHandicraft typeface. Each of those is a different font.

With a high-resolution laser printer, say 600 dots per inch, you can have as many fonts as you ~~wish~~ can afford. There are also **scaleable fonts**, which the computer or printer can convert to any size you want, from big headlines to legal fine print.

With some of the DTP software packages and printers, you can rotate the type, use 3-D looking letters, have them cast shadows, put polka dots or plaid patterns inside the letters, or marbleize the type. One could really go wild. (See the next page.)

Another neat thing available to the would-be publisher is **clip art**. These are images that have been scanned, and the resulting digitized images copied onto disks which you can buy. You then select one or several images and add them to your publication. To include one in your document, you use the mouse to select it, use the mouse again to mark the spot where you want it, and then "click" on an icon to "paste" the image at that spot. The icon is usually a paste pot, naturally. And there is a scissors icon for cutting something out.

With all this at your disposal, you can use the computer to make up newsletters which you might print on your laser printer, or prepare copy ready to send to a commercial print shop (skipping the typesetter).

There's only one catch to this desk top publishing. To create a high quality page layout you need experience and some talent as a graphics designer. Having **all** *these* fonts **does** not mean you know how **to** use them *artistically*.

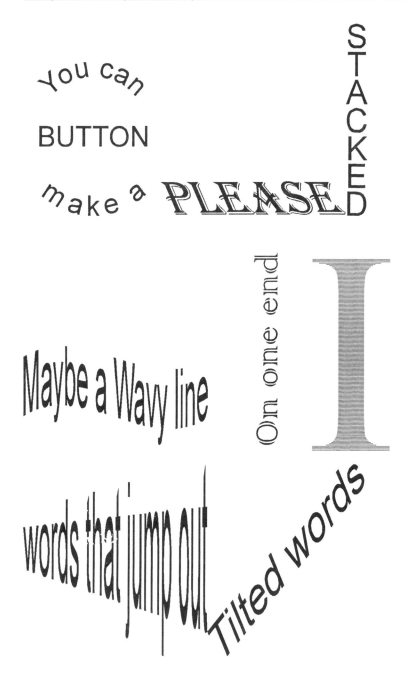

You can

BUTTON

make a PLEASE

STACKED

On one end

I

Maybe a Wavy line

words that jump out

Tilted words

A smooth operator

With so much stuff involved, there has to be a controlling mechanism. In a computer, that mechanism is the Operating System, or OS. It runs the show. It is the first thing loaded into memory when you turn the computer on. It manages all the jobs; it keeps track of what's happening with the disks and peripherals; it handles security if needed. Simply put, the **Operating System** is a program which manages the resources of the computer system.

The operating system has a tougher job if more than one thing is running at the same time. This is called **multitasking**. On a single micro,  multitasking is **timesharing**. It works just like timesharing a condo in Acapulco. Almost. Instead of one week a year, its one **Tick** (that's 1/18 of a second, not a varmint on your dog) out of every second. Or some other arrangement that the manager has set up—which might depend on how close you are with the manager. (Still sounds like the condo deal.)

In the computer's case, it's the OS that keeps everything on schedule. It must see that each task gets time, though not necessarily equal amounts. And it's smart. If it observes that some program is not using all of its assigned time slot (for instance, a user is typing), it will use that idle time for other work.

Wait a minute, you say. What idle time? I'm a fast typist. However fast you are, the computer is faster. If you were typing at 60 words a minute (with or without errors), the computer would be idle more than 99% of the time! If you paused for 1 second to turn the page, the computer could do literally thousands of things. If another job were running, a good OS would utilize that second to do a lot of things.

The OS must also keep track of data. When you (or a program) ask for data stored on the disk, you don't know where that piece of data is stored. The OS, like a reference librarian, uses a program called a **disk driver** to find it for you.

For micros, the most widely used operating system is called **DOS**, for **D**isk **O**perating **S**ystem. Different companies sell versions of DOS, so you have **PC-DOS, MS-DOS, DR DOS, PC-MOS**, and others. Windows, which we discussed earlier, has not been an operating system, as such, rather an interface between you and DOS. That is about to change and Windows will not need DOS in the future.

This brings up another term, **shell**. For computers, this means we wrap the operating system in a more "User

Friendly" package. We deal with the shell, and the shell deals with the operating system.

OS/2 is an operating system used on IBM's PS/2 computers. The operating system on a **Mac** (the Apple Macintosh) is called **System 7**. It's similar to Windows—and was in use for several years before Windows arrived on the scene.

UNIX, a multitasking OS developed by AT&T 25 years ago, runs on micro computers, minicomputers, and mainframes. Very few operating systems can do that. As with DOS, there are many versions, including several with names built around **XENIX**.

IBM uses **MVS, VM, VSE** and others on its larger machines. **DEC** (**D**igital Equipment Corp.) uses **VMS,** and **ULTRIX** and **OSF** (versions of Unix) and others.

There must be at least a hundred operating systems. They all do basically the same thing: manage the show.

Alphabet soup: CAD, CAE, CAM and CASE

CAD, CAM, CAE, and CASE are areas of computer work and generally refer to software packages.

Since computers were first used for mathematical calculations, it is reasonable to believe that engineers would make use of them. **Computer Aided Design**, or **CAD**, is one way. The computer provides the tools to make the original design—of almost anything—much, much easier. But it's most useful when the boss or client wants a change. Before CAD, even a small change might have been a lot of work. With CAD, it's not.

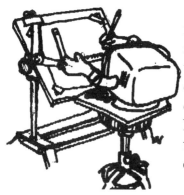

Suppose one component in the middle of a complex drawing needs to be shifted one inch to the right. That means everything to the right of that component must shift also. Nothing will do but to redraw the entire design. But if the drawing was made on a CAD system, you can simply tell the computer to shift that component, and everything to its right, one inch and then draw a new clean copy for you. You know the computer: give it a command and it does it without complaining.

That's just one simple example. CAD does much more. CAD is sometimes used for **Computer Aided Drafting**. And some packages are called **CADD**, for **Computer Aided Drafting and Design.**

The next step is to let the computer analyze some of the more complicated designs. That's where **Computer Aided Engineering**, or **CAE**, comes in. A CAE program can analyze a CAD design. If it's a building or some other structure, then a CAE system can do a structural analysis of it. In a similar fashion, CAD and CAE programs can be used on electronic circuit boards—or the design of IC's. Most airplanes and all computers are tested and analyzed with CAE programs to find problems before even the first prototype is built.

Suppose a product is designed and checked using computer aided systems, and the manufacturing of the product is also automated. With **Computer Aided Manufacturing** pro-grams or **CAM**, the design from the CAD system (which was checked with the CAE system) is passed to the CAM system. The CAM can determine how much raw material will be needed, check

inventory for its availability, determine the time needed to complete the job, schedule production according to availability of the machines needed, and design the programs that will drive the machines to produce the product. It will then reduce the inventory by the amount used, and print out the required paperwork. All without a coffee break!

But will it wash windows?

If they help architects and engineers, you'd think that the computer people would make some tools to help themselves. They have, although those tools are not as advanced as the ones for engineering. **Computer Aided Software Engineering**, or **CASE**, lets the computer help the programmer write the programs which will tell the computer what to do.

Sounds like a conflict of interest to me.

Escape, control and hot stuff!

There are a few special keys whose names computer people, and fiction writers, throw around. You can catch them (the people, not the keys) off guard by knowing what those names mean.

The **escape key** has nothing to do with Steve McQueen breaking out of the prison camp. It is not the secret to  Houdini's great tricks. **Escape**, or **ESC**, as it is sometimes written, is often used to do just that—escape. You're in a place in a computer program that you don't want to be in. How do you get out? Frequently, you simply press (that's like hit, but seems gentler for the keyboard) the escape key.

The escape key is also used to start some special sequence of key strokes, called (now this is really clever) an **escape sequence**. You want the computer to recognize that the key strokes coming next are to be considered in a special fashion—they will mean something different from what they usually do. Escape sequences are often sent to the printer, for instance. By preceding the string with the escape, the printer knows that what follows are instructions on *how* to print, rather than something to print. As an example, ESC &l2D tells a Hewlett Packard LaserJet to double space the printing, not to actually print an & or a l or a 2 or a D.

The **control key**, often written as **CTRL**, is used in conjunction with another key to change the meaning of that other key. For instance, holding down the control key and then pressing the letter P might tell the computer that you want to turn the printer on, not that you want to type the letter P. You add additional "control".

Here's a hot item: many programs define what they call a **hot key**. When you press it, the computer does some special thing, or activates some program, no matter what else is going on at that time. For example, you can set up a TSR program (we discussed "Terminate and Stay Resident" in the Hardware, Software chapter) that keeps a calculator lurking in the background. Whenever you hit the special hot key for that TSR, the calculator will pop up, regardless of what else you might have been doing. So you want to select the hot key with care. It wouldn't do to make the space bar the hot key.

All of these are simply ways to make life easier. I'm all for that.

Tasty leftovers

There are a bunch of terms that are important—and interesting—that just didn't fit in before. I could leave them out. But I think they ought to be here in case you're interested.

I will try to make these **user friendly**. In the computer world, "User Friendly" means something easier has been put between us and the natural difficulty of the computer. Sort of like a saddle. The horse may be a friend. But his natural bone structure is not necessarily very compatible with *our* bone structure.

Bulletin boards are suppose to make life easier. Nowadays, a **Bulletin Board Service**, or **BBS**, means a computer-based

version of the traditional cork board. It works pretty much like the old cork boards, but you can access it with your computer from anywhere, via telephone lines.

When a person in the Northeast is "on line" that means he is standing in a line of people. To a computer person, **on line** simply means connected to a computer. It may be permanent or temporary. But the basic idea is the same: connected.

Another computer term that has to do with connected (at least loosely) is **bundled**. It refers to programs (software) that are included "at no extra charge" when a computer or larger software package is purchased. These extra goodies are "bundled in" or connected with the larger item, much like the "extra value" packages on new cars. Do you believe that "no extra charge" bit? I didn't think so.

Which leads us to **cache**, pronounced like "cash". For computers, cache is used two ways: 1) as special memory that is much faster than regular memory (and costs more), and 2) as a part of regular memory that works with the disk, making the disk seem faster than it actually is. To put this in perspective, the disk does things in thousandths of seconds while memory operates in millionths of seconds. Roughly speaking, memory is ten thousand times faster than a fast disk for certain operations. So, memory could certainly help the disks look better.

Double density, like Doublemint gum, gives you twice as much pleasure. A 5¼" diskette might hold 360,000 characters (Single Density)—not used much any more, 720,000 (Double Density) or 1,200,000 characters (High Density). Depends on how the disk was manufactured and **formatted** (prepared to receive data). On 3½" diskettes, you can get 720,000 characters (single density) or 1.44 million (double density). That's not backwards. The smaller disks do hold more. That's because the smaller ones are newer technology.

I heard someone ask what those numbers mean. Well, the 5¼" diskettes will hold roughly 200, 400 or 650 typed pages of information, depending on the density of the diskette. For the 3½" diskettes, the numbers would be about 400 and 800 pages.

The outside packaging of the diskettes are roughly square and the size in inches refers to the length of one side. They're thin, about 1/8" thick. The 5¼" is in a flexible plastic envelope while the 3½" is in a hard plastic case. So, with the 3½", you can slip the equivalent of 800 pages of information in your shirt pocket. There are programs which **pack** data, that is, encode it more densely than normal. (When using one such program, **Pkzip**, computer people say they "**zipped**" the data.) Packing the data, you might get as many as 2,000 pages on one 3½" diskette. Great for spy stories.

Footprint makes me think of Big Foot. To computer people, **footprint** immediately brings to mind how much space on the desk, or floor, the computer takes. (Big Foot is certainly more interesting!)

If you guessed that a **microsecond** is a small second, you're right. A microsecond is actually one-millionth of a second. Not nearly as long as the blink of an eye or the shake of a lamb's tail. But MUCH longer than a **nanosecond**, which is only one thousandth as long as a microsecond, or one billionth of a second. Computers actually do things in microseconds, and in a few nanoseconds. Sort of like you and me—when we were younger, of course.

Ribbon cable is not a cable in satin or grosgrain. It is a cable consisting of anywhere from four to 64 wires, laying side by side in one flat, wide ... ah ... ribbon. Each wire will carry a particular signal, or electric current. The plug for the cable has to have as many prongs (or sockets) as there are wires. But don't worry, they're small, so the cable doesn't get too big to fit inside the computer.

Screen saver. If the exact same picture stayed on your monitor or terminal for a long time, it would "burn in" that image on the phosphorus of the tube. From then on, that picture would be there like a faint shadow on your screen. Of course, if you turn your CRT off whenever you're not using it, that won't happen. But sometimes you go away and forget it; or intend to be back soon and aren't. There are TSR programs that check on this. If they find that nothing has happened on the CRT for some time, they hop right in. Now, they could just blank the screen—and some do. But the more inventive ones put up pictures that constantly change (hence, no burning in). Some have fish swimming around, or fireworks, or frogs or toasters with wings flying around or ... whatever one can imagine. "Burn in" is not much of a problem with the newer monitors, but the screen savers are fun, inexpensive and people like them.

On a **Multitasking** system, you could be running a program doing some calculations in the **background** (out of sight) while you are using a word processor in the **foreground** (what you are watching on the screen).

Wild card. This could mean a funny character who goes a little overboard. Or a special card in a poker game, as in "Let's play one-eyed jacks are wild". But for the computer community it generally means that any letter or combination of letters can be used in place of the wild card character. Often the * is used for the wild card. So if you asked the computer to show the names of files that match *USER**, you could get *USER1* and *USERTWO* and *USERJIM* and *USERJANE* and *USER*.

Telecommunications refers to the entire field of electronic transmission of information, whether data between computers, sound over telephone wires, TV, Fax, etc.

A **Bus** on a computer is a path on which data travels.

A **Cell** is a term used in spread sheet programs to mean the intersection of one row with one column, where one piece of data can be stored and accessed by giving the row and column numbers.

Booting up the machine is simply starting it up. Maybe that's as in kick-start it, or give it a boot. A **cold boot** means starting it when the power is off. A **warm boot** means that the power is still on and you simply want to get a new copy of the operating system loaded into memory and start from scratch, but without turning the power off. (This is easier on the machine than getting a jolt of electricity surging through its veins.) Remember what I said about the computer people not wanting us to know what they're talking about? They could have said "start from off" and "restart while on." But then we'd know what they were talking about.

I was ready to stop, but I'm getting flack from the worm. It feels that the mouse got a lot of press and it wants equal time. So, in the interest of fairness in broadcasting, I give you the WORM.

WORM stands for **W**rite **O**nce **R**ead **M**any times. Remember the CD-ROM disks? They are WORM drives. Somebody writes the data on there, but one shot is all they get. However, you (well, really it's the computer) can read the disk as often as you like. Not a bad deal. For instance, they put an encyclopedia on a WORM. You can access it all you want. And you don't have to worry about accidentally writing over it; you can't. And one CD-ROM disk can contain an entire set of encyclopedias.

So, like the mouse, to a computer a WORM is a wonderful thing.

Would you RISC a RAID?

onsider this a brief glossary, a map of the maze of acronyms and jargon computer people use. When a friend or a book throws one of these at you, you'll have this chapter for your catcher's mitt.

ASCII - (pronounced ask-ee) is short for **A**merican **S**tandard 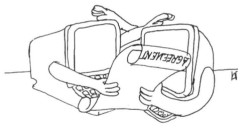 **C**ode for **I**nformation **I**nterchange. It means a lot of people agreed on how to code things. (Remember the secret decoder ring—it still lives!) At any rate, this lets us write data to a disk in a form other people can read on their computers. Basically, it's a universal language.

BPS: stands for **B**its **P**er **S**econd, how many bits are passing by per second. **Baud** means roughly the same.

Clock speed. Think of this as the metronome for the computer. A quartz crystal sends out pulses, like it does in a quartz watch. These are used to precisely regulate the timing for the computer.

Clock doubling: a process whereby a microcomputer can double the speed with which it handles things internally, while still operating at its regular speed when dealing with peripherals. That's like your working very fast at the office, but slowing down when you interact with other people. Some Intel 80486, or simply 486, chips can do this. This speeds some of your work, but not all.

CMOS is short for **C**omplementary **M**etal **O**xide Semiconductor. It is a variation of **MOS.** Both are design methods for producing semiconductors.

COMDEX is the largest trade show in America. COMDEX stands for **COM**puter **D**ealers **EX**position. It started in 1979 and attracted about 4,000 attendees. There are now fall and spring versions. Just to give you an idea of how this industry has grown, the COMDEX/Fall 1994 drew 190,000 attendees!

CP/M was the predecessor to DOS. An operating system for microcomputers.

If a computer user says he lost his FAT, do not congratulate him; it doesn't mean he's gotten skinny. It means he's got real problems. In a computer, the **FAT** is the **F**ile **A**llocation **T**able. This FAT is necessary if the computer is going to find all those files written on the disk. If it's lost, it is either very difficult or impossible to find the files on the disk. Not good.

4GL: stands for **4**th **G**eneration **L**anguage First generation languages use machine instructions. Second generation languages are still machine dependent, but have some niceties. Third generation languages are considered high-level languages and are machine independent. 4GL's include some query languages, report writers and some others. They're supposed to let us enter commands closer to the way *we* talk than the way the computer wants it. Y'all git it, huh?

Glitch: when the program trips on a bug.   Usually not a serious bug.   Also refers to a very brief interruption in electrical power.

GIGO: **G**arbage **I**n, **G**arbage **O**ut. (Pronounced Guy-Go.) If your input is trash, the output can't be any better.

MIPS: Don't get miffed over MIPS.   It simply means **M**illions of **I**nstructions **P**er **S**econd.   It's a measure of machine speed.

MegaFLOPS: Would you believe a really big flop? Like a

play that cost millions of dollars and closed after opening night? Or certain government programs? For computers, it means **M**illions of **FL**oating point **O**perations **P**er **S**econd. Still a different way to measure machine speed. (**Floating Point** means numbers with decimal points in them.)

Megahertz: one of the most commonly used terms for computer speed. It's a measure of how fast the CPU operates. Five years ago, 25 megahertz was very fast. Today, 100 is considered speedy for a micro. But they're demonstrating micros operating at 150 and 200 megahertz. That's six to eight times faster than the 25 megahertz machine—if the rest of the stuff can keep up. No guarantee there. Some mainframes currently run at 275 megahertz, and probably higher by the time you read this.

RAID stands for **R**edundant **A**rray of **I**nexpensive **D**isks. A RAID is several disks that store data so if one fails, its data can still be recovered. Not everyone thinks it's inexpensive.

RISC is a **R**educed **I**nstruction **S**et **C**omputer. A computer without all its marbles? Not exactly. These are special-purpose computers that don't need a full set of instructions. But they can be used for general purpose situations. Since they are usually very fast, they may be able to "get around" the lack of an instruction, doing several things to accomplish the missing instruction, as quickly as having the full set. IBM's POWERstation is an example of a RISC machine.

Tower or **Tower Case** - This is a biggy. It means instead of the computer sitting horizontally, it stands on its end

UPS - **U**ninterruptible **P**ower **S**upply, or United Parcel Service, if you're not into computers. Really means you've got a back-up system in case the regular power fails. The UPS will keep it running through short power outages. And if the power stays off, it gives time to shut down in an orderly fashion. A small glitch in the electricity can cause big problems in the computer. The reason is simple. A refrigerator plods along. And if the electric current is cut for half a second, it won't even see it. But in that length of time, the computer could have executed thousands of instructions. So, that glitch will make the computer very unhappy, possibly requiring a service call to get it back running.

And tomorrow?

Looking into the crystal ball is tough in the computer industry. By the time you write down your predictions for the future, they're already being sold. But certain things are inevitable. Smaller and faster. At all levels. Gigabyte disks will be on notebook computers which will run at 300 megahertz. True motion video, in true color, will be available on everything and improved compression routines will drastically cut the disk space required for it. Video conferencing will get down to less than $1,000 and become as standard as a fax is today. Faxes and modems will actually *achieve* a 56K bit through-put. And maybe fast, true-color laser printing will get down to an affordable price.

The biggest wonder is that some installations will finally work smoothly. Not *every* time, of course. Grid-lock will cause the Iway to become a system of Iways. But access to the Iways will become common place, and computer "guides" and "assistants" will make finding things easy. Voice input will become less sensitive to accents, whether regional or foreign, and allow for continuous speech. Voice prints will help improve security. Hal, of "2001" fame, will be a reality. However, voice stress problems will replace today's carpal tunnel syndrome as the hazard of the workplace. And computers will learn to recognize gestures and know if you're being polite.

Artificial Intelligence will gain greater respect. A wide variety of programs will analyze data of all sorts and make decisions that are accepted. In addition, they will solve a variety of problems that are either ignored today, or take time from humans that could be used for other things. Computers will catch design flaws much more regularly, and at a much earlier stage to improve efficiency and cut costs in many diverse areas. (Hopefully, they will be able to catch some of the bugs in commercial software packages.)

Information retrieval and AI will join forces to allow us to find what we want no matter where it is and quickly.

With expanded wireless transmission capability, you will be able to access data bases, send e-mail, buy and sell almost anything, and carry out other business transactions from anywhere—in the park, or floating in the middle of a lake. And your e-cash will be safe.

And perhaps there will even be a CULAC: Computer Users' Legal Aid Committee.

If you've gotten through all this, *and didn't start at the back*, then you are computer literate. You know as much, or more, than most of the people using computers. I know, you haven't plugged in memory modules, changed the CMOS settings or checked the IRQ. I didn't say you were a computer expert. But you are certainly computer literate. And not a stuffed shirt about it, I hope.

But, as the wizard said to the scarecrow in Oz "... they have one thing you haven't got—a diploma." So, please go to the next page.

Diploma
of
Computer Literacy

---

is hereby awarded this

Diploma of Computer Literacy

having successfully completed the

Bits, Bytes, Apples and Mice

Computer Literacy equivalency course.

Signed this ___ day of _____,
19___

C. Mouse

Joy Stick

C. Mouse   Joy Stick

APPENDIX

How do we translate 1995 from our familiar decimal system into 11111001011 in a binary system?

First, how does the decimal system that we use work? In the decimal system, each place gets multiplied by a power of 10 (a decimal system is based on 10). So, for example, 7503 becomes:

$$3 \times 10^{**}0 = 3 \times 1 \qquad = \qquad 3$$
$$0 \times 10^{**}1 = 0 \times 10 \qquad = \qquad 0$$
$$5 \times 10^{**}2 = 5 \times 100 \qquad = \qquad 500$$
$$7 \times 10^{**}3 = 7 \times 1000 \qquad = \qquad 7000$$

$$\overline{\qquad 7503}$$

It's the same thing in binary, except that you use powers of 2 instead of powers of 10. To get the 1995 you need 11111001011 because:

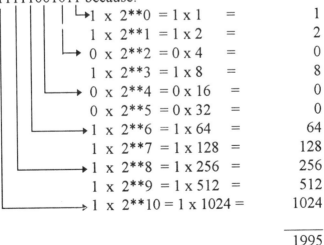

1 x 2**0 = 1 x 1	=	1
1 x 2**1 = 1 x 2	=	2
0 x 2**2 = 0 x 4	=	0
1 x 2**3 = 1 x 8	=	8
0 x 2**4 = 0 x 16	=	0
0 x 2**5 = 0 x 32	=	0
1 x 2**6 = 1 x 64	=	64
1 x 2**7 = 1 x 128	=	128
1 x 2**8 = 1 x 256	=	256
1 x 2**9 = 1 x 512	=	512
1 x 2**10 = 1 x 1024	=	1024

$$\overline{\qquad 1995}$$

Note: 10**3 = 10 x 10 x 10. Similarily, 2**4 = 2 x 2 x 2 x 2.

Index

Order Form

☎ Telephone orders: Call (903) 365-7152. Have your VISA or MasterCard ready.   * Fax orders: (903) 342 - 5803

✍ Postal orders: Pennant Publishing, Thelma Shewmaker, P.O. Drawer #25, Winnsboro, Texas 75494-0025.

Please send the items checked:

Computer Literacy Made Easy ... And Fun

❑ _____Copies of book @ $12.95 each.

❑ _____Copies of Cassette @ $16.95 each.

❑ _____Copies of **Certificate of Computer Literacy** @$9.95 each -- Suitable for framing and signed by Mr. Callan personally. (Send name(s) _typed_ to insure correct spelling on certificate(s).

Name:_____

Address: _____

City:_____ State: _____Zip: _____

Telephone: (____)_____

Sales Tax: Please add 7.75% for items shipped to Texas addresses.

Shipping: Book rate: $2.50 for the first item and 75 cents for each additional item (Surface shipping may take three to four weeks.) Second day shipping $4.50 per item.

Payment: ❑ Check   ❑ VISA   ❑ MasterCard

Total Amount: U.S. $ _____

Card Number: _____Exp. Date: _____

Name on card: _____

Order Form

☎ Telephone orders: Call (903) 365-7152. Have your VISA or MasterCard ready.   * Fax orders: (903) 342 - 5803

✍ Postal orders: Pennant Publishing, Thelma Shewmaker, P.O. Drawer #25, Winnsboro, Texas 75494-0025.

Please send the items checked:
Computer Literacy Made Easy ... And Fun
❑ _____Copies of book @ $12.95 each.
❑ _____Copies of Cassette @ $16.95 each.
❑ _____Copies of **Certificate of Computer Literacy** @$9.95 each -- Suitable for framing and signed by Mr. Callan personally. (Send name(s) _typed_ to insure correct spelling on certificate(s).

Name:_____

Address: _____

City:_____ State: _____Zip: _____

Telephone: (_____)_____
Sales Tax: Please add 7.75% for items shipped to Texas addresses.

Shipping: Book rate: $2.50 for the first item and 75 cents for each additional item (Surface shipping may take three to four weeks.) Second day shipping $4.50 per item.

Payment: ❑ Check   ❑ VISA   ❑ MasterCard

Total Amount: U.S. $ _____

Card Number: _____Exp. Date: _____

Name on card: _____